LIFE
MAPS

LIFE MAPS

CONVERSATIONS ON THE JOURNEY OF FAITH

James W. Fowler
Sam Keen

Edited by JEROME W. BERRYMAN

WORD BOOKS
PUBLISHER
WACO, TEXAS

A DIVISION OF
WORD, INCORPORATED

Life-Maps:
Conversations on the Journey of Faith
James Fowler and Sam Keen
edited by Jerome Berryman

Library of Congress Catalog Card Number: 76.58741
ISBN: 0–8499–0493–5
ISBN: 0–8499–3029–4 (paperback)
Printed in the United States of America

567898 MV 987654321

Contents

Acknowledgments

It gives me great pleasure to express publicly my gratitude to the many people who helped make this book. The supporters and directors of the following foundations deserve primary recognition because they funded the conference out of which the book grew: the Comprehensive Services for Education (CSE); the Diocese of Galveston-Houston; Interface; the National Conference of Christians and Jews; the Presbytery of Brazos; the Therapeutic Intervention Program for Children (TIPS); and the Henderson-Wessendorff Foundation.

At the Institute of Religion, the directors, Julian Byrd and then Ron Sunderland, willingly lent their enthusiasm to the project. The whole faculty and the Board, in fact, were a continual source of inspiration and support. To Dr. Kenneth Vaux, Professor of Medical Ethics, who has been especially generous with his consistent affirmation and critical judgment over my years at the Institute, I owe a special debt.

The task of getting the conference tapes onto paper and

then moving through several drafts toward a final manuscript was greatly eased by Francis Carter, Audrey Laymance, and Weir Smith. Their competence, patience, and suggestions are much appreciated.

Sam Keen and Jim Fowler have been wonderful to work with. Their creativity, discipline, and deep commitment to their work, and to people have been a constantly renewing leaven. I have enjoyed the differences in their personalities as well as the consistencies.

To Thea I would like to say thank you for being yourself and for being with me as a wife. To our children, Alyda and Coleen, I would like to say thank you for being with us and for being two such special and unique human beings. Without the support and understanding of our small "multitude," the book would have remained only talk.

Audrey Laymance helped prepare the second edition for publication, as she did with the first edition. As always, it was a pleasure to work with her and to work with an old friend of this book. The Director of the Institute of Religion during the period of preparation was Dr. David L. Stitt, who was a sustaining and challenging comfort to the editor. My thanks to him for this and for many things cannot go unrecorded here.

Jerome W. Berryman
The Institute of Religion, 1984

Life-Maps:

Conversations on the Journey of Faith

Introduction to the Second Edition

Anyone alive lives by faith. It is what keeps us going when love has turned to hate or hope to despair. Faith helps us carry on when there is no longer any reason to go forward. It enables us to exist during the in-between times: between meanings, amid dangers of radical discontinuity, even in the face of death. Faith is the *sine qua non* of life, a primal force we cannot do without.

This book explores faith by presenting a conversation between two people equally fascinated by faith, but they approach this phenomenon from very different points of view. Jim Fowler examines the developmental structure of "faith as knowing" and analyzes what happens when our way of knowing changes. Sam Keen looks at the developmental aspect of faith's force as trust and at what happens when that force is frustrated and damned by being dammed up.

The conversation of this book began a live and lively dialogue at the Institute of Religion in the Texas Medical Center in Houston. That conversation of 10 May 1975, withstood second and third thoughts, editorial changes, our first publisher going out of business, the coordination of three complicated schedules and the welcome invitation of Word Books. Books were shipped to booksellers on 3 November 1978, almost two and one half years after the colloquium.

It was worth the wait and the work. *Life Maps* has proven itself to be a useful book to many. The first edition went through four printings before being sold completely out. This second edition was suggested by the publisher, because of the interest and conversation the book still stimulates.

The second edition has been prepared with few changes in the main body of the book. There has been some work on the format and most of the misprints have been caught. One area has been changed. The editor has added a rather long postscript to the book to focus on the interplay among the two authors and the reader.

The authors of *Life Maps* did not intend their presentations to be considered as finished statements of their faith models. Both treated this situation as a good place to try out new ideas in a near-final state of preparation. Both suggested that a more formal and final statement would be forthcoming after 1978. Both authors have been true to their word.

Jim Fowler's major faith development book, *Stages of Faith: The Psychology of Human Development and the Quest for Meaning,*[1] appeared in 1981. Sam Keen's book, *The Passionate Life: Stages of Loving,*[2] was published in 1983.

The question about whether faith is essentially a quest for meaning or a quest for an authentic life of love is not a new one in the history of theology. Centuries of debates echo in these pages, but they are not our primary concern. The main point of this book is to be faithful to the conversation about faith in order to enable it to continue and progress.

This book is based on the idea that faith studies are not

ruled by the myth of Sisyphus. This conversation is not like rolling the same boulder up a hill only to have it roll back down again. This book lives squarely in the hopeful knowledge and love that we not only have to reinvent the faith conversation in each generation but that any generation has the possibility of genuine discovery as it maps faith for its time and place. One never knows when the dimension of a new frontier will emerge from human experience and reflection.

Paul Tillich drew on 71 years of experience when he published *Dynamics of Faith*.[3] He resisted the temptation to throw out the word, "faith," altogether. He decided to attempt to "heal" the word rather than exile it as the death-of-God theologians did with the word, "God."

Life Maps is intended to help continue healing the word, "faith," but not by rendering a definitive statement of its meaning. The goal here is to awaken the dormant and often dull conversation by presenting the stories of true explorers who have returned from their journeys with new information and excitement about faith.

Another faith explorer, H. Richard Niebuhr, was working on a major book about faith when he died. Jim Fowler studied that manuscript and wrote his first book, *To See the Kingdom*,[4] published in 1974, about it.

Niebuhr struggled with the definition of faith. He suggested that it might have multiple and unrelated meanings like the word, "organ." It might mean a musical instrument, a part of the body, or a newspaper. The word cannot disclose itself. It depends on its context for definition.

Tillich added dynamic pushes and pulls to the faith model. Niebuhr speculated about a faith process at work in his model. The complexity of the process was thought to be as complex as the process of reason. "Reason" involves "perception and conception, distinction and relation, experience and abstraction, intuition and inference, and contemplation and measurement," he said.

H. Richard Niebuhr, Fowler's theological mentor, was one of the earliest of the theologians to see how the process of knowing identified by Michael Polanyi could reframe the relationship between religion and science so that both sides could be responsible and faithful. He called Polanyi a "moral philosopher" because he took responsibility for his knowledge and expressed his views so that the role of faith in science and society might be better understood and used.

Fowler and Keen add the dimension of a developmental process to the movement away from a static picture of faith led by Tillich and Niebuhr.

The developmental perspective implies that faith changes and yet paradoxically it remains somewhat the same. Faith is like a journey. A person remains the same person in enough ways to be recognized but he or she might have been at the same time greatly changed by the trip.

Life Maps is a book that plays with the metaphor of the journey and of mapping the journey. In the new chapter at the end of the book there will be a discussion also of mapping the maps themselves. Before turning to the presentation of Fowler and Keen and their dialogue, a few more general words need to be said about the journey of faith in the context of our time.

The Life/Faith Journey

The very ancient and broadly used image of the *Journey* is our common metaphor for living. We form and reform who we are as persons making our way. Each generation produces and leaves behind it a literature of concern about this journey. Evidence of such "faith maps" is, in fact, strewn about us from every century and from every part of the earth.[5]

Lao Tzu talked of the *Tao*, which in one translation has been translated as the Way. Buddhists speak of the *Mahayana*, which is translated as the Great Way. Hindus refer to the *Deva-yana*, or the Way of the Gods. Christ said, "I am the Way." Moses showed the people of Israel the way out of bondage into the Promised Land. In Islam, the Prophet Mohammed led the Way to Mecca. There is the *sirat al-mustaquim*, sometimes translated as the Straight Way, and there is the Sufic *tariqah*, or Way. The Straight Way is the theme in both the Psalms and the Gospels. The Sioux trod the Red Road and the Japanese sought the *Shodo*, or Holy Path.

In addition to the images in words and art, the inner journey of the self has often had geographical places associated with it. In a blending of inner and outer travel, for instance, pilgrims have trod toward Jerusalem, Mecca, Lhasa, Benares, and Rome. They have gone to the mountains and deserts as well as to the cities. They have undertaken quests for the Holy Grail, the Terrestrial Paradise, or for the Fountain of Eternal Youth. Voyages have been made in search of sacred isles of peace, the Golden Fleece, or the way home. The Papacy even retained the symbols of the key and the bark despite their former association with the pagan god Janus, long before St. Peter. Their power was evident, for we are all on the way from dust to dust.

Today it is much easier than ever before, especially for a North American, to journey to places reputed to be holy. Spiritual journeys, on the other hand, have become more difficult. Timetables stand in our way. Spiritual journeys require a sensitivity to *being in the present*. Our attention to the past or to the future or to coordinating the schedules of people and time zones, however, seems to squeeze out the present. Although the image of the journey is universal, most of us in the airways or on the freeways are not on the way to the freedom from past and future that is necessary before we can experience the quality of faith's *present*. The cartography of faith is always difficult and complex. But today our being taught to be absent from the present compounds the difficulties! Faith is more difficult to feel, to develop, even to imagine today—let alone to discuss.

A work called *Divani Shamsi Tabriz*, attributed to Jalal al-Din Rumi, the great eleventh-century Sufi poet and founder of the Mevlevi Order of dervishes, says, in part, "You failed to go on the pilgrimage because of your ass's nature, not because you have no ass." Our inability to be in the present and our failure to see faith's reality contribute to a change of nature that slows or stops the pilgrim's journey. In the flurry of outer journeys, the inner journey fades. There is a winding down of faith's creative force.

The visualization of faith is an experience. It is not a thought, a concept, or a deduction. Visualization involves participation. There is a feeling of union with what is being visualized or with people visualizing in common. With our eyes open, we see by means of light. With our eyes closed, we rely on previous vision to translate for our imagination. In either case, we have been taught what to notice as significant. The photochemical reaction in the eye triggers nerve impulses that eventually are conducted to the visual area of the brain's cerebral cortex. The visual area registers electrical stimuli received from the retina as meaningless patterns of light. People blind from birth whose sight is restored through surgery only perceive light. The images by which we connect the inner and outer worlds to make sense of our journey have to be learned. We have to have our attention called to them. What we have been taught about faith and the means of grace, whether by intention or by default, greatly determines the "eye" we have for faith.

Sartre was right. Many of us try to pretend our wishes into existence and call that process faith. That type of faith is counterfeit. So also is faith derived from irresponsible evidence. On the other hand, one can go too far in avoiding counterfeit faith. Roquentin in Sartre's book *Nausea*, for example, looks toward the sea and observes: "The *true* sea is cold and black, full of animals; it crawls under this thin green film made to deceive human beings."[6] That, too, is partial vision. One wishes Roquentin might discover Sald al-Din Mahmud Shabistari (d. 1320) on the beach and consider with him another case. In the *Mystic Rose Garden*, he says: "Do not seek with cold eyes to find blemishes./Or the roses will turn to thorns as you gaze."

Seeing is the crux of the matter. In this book, the tools for seeing, the maps, are made explicit. We are not talking about seeing with cold or hot eyes; we are talking about entering a circle where one "trusts through knowing and knows through trusting." It is also this seeming paradox that Keen and Fowler explore.

The Long Way Around to Faith Today

I believe that insensitivity to faith is part of a larger problem, a deeper numbness. We are victims of overstimulation. The bombardment of the senses, information overload, and stress from constant decision-making cause us to move from fatigue to hypersensitivity and overreaction to emotional exhaustion to, literally, a deep psychological and spiritual numbness.

Protection comes at first in the form of bad faith. We try to recast the past and to deny the future in a variety of forms. Finally, we deny the past, present, and future, and ultimately the self. Alvin Toffler catalogues some personalities living in the domain of bad faith. Such "victims of future shock" are: the "Denier," who blocks out all unwelcome reality, denying its existence; the "Specialist," who blocks out all change except that within his own specialty; the "Reversionist," who dogmatically reverts to the past to face the future; and the "Super-Simplifier," who counts on the quick answers of the latest fad to distract from the future.[7]

Religion is about "biosocial continuity," about life in the face of death. It is about confronting "living deadness" and evoking new life. It is filled with the images we need for psychic nourishment; but, as Robert Lifton has pointed out in *The Life of the Self,* "The quest for images and symbols in new combination, for what might be called communal re-symbolization, is precarious and threatening—so much so that it can itself be falsely viewed as the cause for the cultural breakdown everyone senses."[8] Religious leaders have been no more immune to overstimulation and the discontinuity of change than anyone else. The Denier, the Specialist, the Reversionist, and the Super-Simplifier are quite at home in parish and seminary.

There are signs of change everywhere, but they are coming the long way around to Western religion. Lifton's book suggests recent change in the formulation of the paradigm of psychological science to include death and continuity. Others, such as Robert E. Ornstein, have helped expand the scope of psychology to include consciousness again. Another door was nudged ajar when *Scientific American* articles from 1954 to 1972 were collected under the title *Altered States of Awareness.*[9] The *Harvard Business Review* carried an article for its readers called "Your Innate Asset for Combating Stress,"[10] which contained a coy little "Appendix" filled with religious language, amid articles on the "Case of Big Mac's Pay Plans" and the "Expanding Scope of SEC Disclosure Laws." Finally, in addition to these signals from psychology, business, and scientific circles, *Powers of the Mind* [11] was made a Book of the Month Club selection, whence it went forth into the world to compete with television images and other distractions from the mind that are customarily available in every home. Religion as "useful" or "different" crept into the West via the back door.

Many have made the journey the long way round *back* to their own Western tradition. Scanning the *Upanishads*, the *Bhagavad Gita*, the works of Sri Ramakrishna, looking into the "Diamond Sutra," pouring over the pages of the *Zenda-vesta*, reading the *Quran*, absorbing Sufi mystical poets, thinking about the *Analects* of Confucius, or reading in the Taoist scriptures—they have come home. A journey through the global domain of faith not only can make what has been invisible in one's own tradition become visible; such a trip can also show that there are good and bad gurus and good and bad ashrams just as there are good and bad spiritual leaders and communities in the West. The rose can be as powerful as the lotus. The cross is a focus as filled with significance as a dot or flame. Faith is itself.

Jalal-uddim Runi (1207-1273) told a story in the *Masnavi*. A man gives a *diram* to each of four persons. The Persian said he would spend his on an *angur*, while the Arab said he would spend his on an *inab*. A Turk said he would spend his on an *uzum*, and a Greek said he would spend his *diram* on an *istabil*. These people began to fight with one another, not knowing that each had in common the desire to purchase a grape.

In the *Meaning and End of Religion*, Wilfred Cantwell Smith pointed out that "In every human community on earth today there exists something that we, as sophisticated observers, may term religion, or a religion. And we are able to see it in each case as the latest development in a continuous tradition that goes back, we can now affirm, for at least one hundred thousand years."[12] In humankind's journey from dust to dust, religion has been central, and the center of religion, where not repressed or distorted, has been the experience and celebration of the process of faith.

In his 1974 Thirkield-Jones Lectures at Gammon Theological Seminary, Jim Fowler referred to a forthcoming book by Smith called *Faith and Belief*. In that book, Smith says: "I for one am inclined to hold that faith, rather than belief, is *a* or *the* fundamental religious category; and that it has usually been so regarded, both in West and East, including classical Christian understanding."[13] An opening up of faith's process again is at the heart of the matter of human health and destiny. A re-seeing of faith will help. A more appropriate map will show the way.

Faith Is Always on the Way

If the discussions of Jim Fowler and Sam Keen seem to go in circles, I would like to suggest that this impression is quite correct. Circularity is appropriate, because it is a part of the nature of faith's process: knowing to trust and trusting to know.

Progress can be made in individual lives as faith winds out in a widening circle of development to include broader ranging, more conscious, and more differentiated kinds of trusting and knowing. Like the development of a child's drawings, faith becomes progressively more detailed and connected in form and force, and more fluent and free in its execution. The image of faith as a knowing-trusting process is certainly not a new idea. Faith contains a "reciprocal causality," as Maurice Blondel called it in his study of St. Augustine.[14] Augustine's use of *crede ut intelligas* and *intellige ut credas* together as a statement of reciprocal causality was no mere confusion or the failure to make a crucial distinction. It is the subtle intuition of faith's deeper process. It is circular and not linear as it spirals upward.

It is significant that Augustine wrote in an age when many felt that the earth was dying. We live that way today, but when Rome fell in 410, the event was tragic to pagan and Christian alike. Rome represented civilization and political stability. St. Jerome said that "the light of the world was put out and the head of the Empire cut off." In 430, Augustine died with the Vandals' siege of his home city, Hippo, raging about him, but the age did not die, and neither will our age die if there is faith. It is by faith that the future is created both in individuals and civilizations.

References: Introduction

1. James W. Fowler, *Stages of Faith* (San Francisco: Harper and Row, 1981).

2. Sam Keen, *The Passionate Life* (San Francisco: Harper and Row, 1983).

3. Paul Tillich, *Dynamics of Faith* (New York: Harper & Brothers, 1957), "Introductory Remarks."

4. H. Richard Niebuhr, "Faith on Earth," unpublished manuscript, chap. 1, "Faith in Question," p. 4, quoted in James W. Fowler, *To See the Kingdom* (Nashville: Abingdon Press, 1974), p. 212.

5. Two general collections of the world's wisdom may be of use to the reader: *The Portable World Bible*, ed. Robert O. Ballou (New York: Viking Press, 1944) compiles "scriptural" texts; *A Treasury of Traditional Wisdom*, ed. Whitall N. Perry (New York: Simon & Schuster, 1971) is arranged in the sequence of a spiritual quest by theme.

6. Jean-Paul Sartre, *Nausea*, trans. (New York: New Directions, 1957), p. 167. *La Nausee* was first published in Paris by Librairie Gallimard in 1938.

7. Alvin Toffler, *Future Shock* (New York: Random House, 1970), pp. 358-364.

8. Robert Jay Lifton, *The Life of the Self* (New York: Simon and Schuster, 1976), p. 135.

9. *Altered States of Awareness: Readings from Scientific American* (San Francisco: W. H. Freeman and Co., 1954-1972), Introduced by Timothy J. Teyler.

10. Herbert Benson, "Your Innate Asset for Combating Stress," *Harvard Business Review*, vol. 52, no. 4 (July-August, 1974), pp. 49-60.

11. Adam Smith, *Powers of Mind* (New York: Random House, 1975).

12. Wilfred Cantwell Smith, *The Meaning and End of Religion* (New York: Mentor Books, 1963), p. 22.

13. Wilfred Cantwell Smith, *Faith and Belief* (in press), quoted in manuscript in James W. Fowler, "Faith, Liberation and Human Development," Lecture I, in *The Foundation* (Atlanta: Gammon Theological Seminary), Vol. 79 (1974), pp. 4-5.

14. Maurice Blondel, "The Latent Resources in St. Augustine's Thought," in *St. Augustine His Age, Life and Thought* (New York:

Meridian Books, 1957), p. 334. See also Paul Ricoeur for a contemporary use of this maxim. He calls it his "hermeneutic circle" of believing and understanding. Paul Ricoeur, *Freud and Philosophy: An Essay on Interpretation*; trans. Dennis Savage (Terry Lecture Series) (New Haven: Yale University Press, 1970), p. 28.

First Presentation:
Jim Fowler*
Life/Faith Patterns:
Structures of Trust & Loyalty

As an introduction to this perspective I would like to share with you three vignettes, without any particular comment upon them at this time. These stories should both give you some clue as to part of my background and also share something of why and how I became interested in studying faith development.

Vignette number one: My father is a Methodist minister. We lived in various towns and communities in western North Carolina as I was growing up. Just after the war, when I was about five, we moved into the mountains in the far western part of that state, to a little community called Spruce Pine where feldspar and mica were mined. During the war the community had been quite prosperous because of the big demand for those products in wartime production. My father worked not only in Spruce Pine, but also with mission churches way out in the mountains in places called Bandanna and Kona.

As a boy of five or six I loved to go with my father on his pastoral calls. Whether talking to merchants and lawyers in Spruce Pine, or to "Uncle Pink" Turbeyfield in the cabin back in the cove, Dad had a way of relating that seemed genuine.

All notes are the author's unless otherwise indicated.

that accepted persons where they were, and that involved adapting his language and style of communication to theirs. As I watched other adults interact with a variety of people, I noticed that not everyone had this capacity. At least not all of them exercised it with my father's obvious care and regard. This striking feature of my father's patterns of communication and caring made a deep impression upon me.

Vignette number two: My first paying job in my early teens was as a garbage man on the maintenance staff of a summer resort. We also hauled brush and limbs, dug ditches, and did a variety of other jobs. I worked with a man in his middle forties whose name was Pete. Pete taught me a lot of things. He taught me how to use what we called an "air-cooled shovel." That is the kind of shovel—hand-operated—with which we dug ditches and water lines. (Let me say in passing that if you have never had the experience of digging a nice, square ditch for a water or sewer line in the red clay soil of western North Carolina, you have missed an esthetic thrill.) What Pete taught me that I valued most, though, was how to drive a truck. One day, as we were returning empty from the garbage dump, we somehow got to discussing a white car that was ahead of us on the road. It soon became apparent that Pete believed that simply because that white car was in front of us, it had to be going faster than we were going. I remarked that it was clear to me that the car was not gaining on us. The distance between us and the car was not widening, nor were we getting closer to it. Therefore, it seemed clear that we were going the same speed. Pete was puzzled by my argument. He insistently contended: "If that car is ahead of us, it has to be going faster than we are going!" After debating this issue fruitlessly for a little while, we finally gave it up.

Vignette number three: This is really less of a story than the other two vignettes. Here I want simply to share the fact that during my first year out of graduate school, in 1968-69, I served as Associate Director of Interpreter's House. This is a center for the continuing education of clergy and for lay retreats in western North Carolina. It is the creation and extension of a great pastor and theologian, Carlyle Marney. During that year at Interpreter's House, I had the privilege of listening to well over two hundred life stories, the stories of people's pilgrimages in faith. We followed a methodological principle there of not giving any lectures or assigning readings until we had heard each person in each of the groups that came, and until we (and they) knew what our agenda needed to be. It was during the course of that agenda-setting that I had the privilege of listening to these life stories.

That year, Erik Erikson's work on the eight stages in the human life cycle became very important to me as a kind of model by which to sort out and organize what I was hearing.[1] I was pretty green coming from graduate school and still talking in footnotes. But in the course of that year, with the help of Erikson's framework, I began to think I could detect certain patterns in people's life stories. I began to discern a typical sequence of transformations, which, despite enormous variety of detail, showed certain formal similarities from person to person. During that year, I now recognize, I was beginning to work out a kind of embryonic theory of religious development. When I returned to Harvard to teach in 1969-70, I was determined to explore that developmental sequence more closely. I resolved to try to provide a context in which contemporary students of theology and future ministers could reflect upon their own processes of development. I wanted to help my students to see their own and others' lives as pilgrimages in faith and as sources for theological construction.

In the course of working with students in those first two

years of teaching, I had some of them ask me, "Do you know the work of Lawrence Kohlberg on moral development?" and "Do you know Kohlberg's critique of Erikson's approach?" A young teacher doesn't get asked that kind of question too often before he makes it his business to become familiar with the material under discussion. I got Kohlberg's writings, met him, and, through that initial exposure, a friendship and collaboration developed. Across the last three years, aided by a generous grant from the Joseph P. Kennedy, Jr. Foundation, my associates and I have begun to investigate life stories more systematically. With their help, I am developing and refining a stage theory of faith development.

To begin, there are four things I want to do. First, I want to share with you the particular way in which we are defining and using the concept of faith as a focus for research. Second, I want to share with you how this focus relates to theories of cognitive and moral development. Third, I want to clarify what we mean when we speak of a structural-developmental perspective on faith. Finally, I want to give you an impressionistic but hopefully reliable set of images by which to understand the stages in the pilgrimage of faith that we have identified.

The Focus on Faith

Several obstacles must be removed before we can use the term *faith* in a way that will serve our purposes. As with other terms which might indicate our focus, faith already carries many connotations. If I asked you to share the ideas about faith which you brought to this reading, perhaps the first meanings that would come to mind would have to do with the religious sphere. Faith and religion are frequently used as synonyms. It may be that "belief" is the term or idea that you would most readily associate with faith. For the purposes of our discussion, however, I want you to think of faith as being both broader and more personal than either religion or belief. Think, if you will, of faith as a *universal*, as a feature of the living, acting, and self-understanding of all human beings, whether they claim to be "believers" or "religious" or not.[2]

For this suggestion to be plausible at all, we must go a bit further in reframing the idea of faith. It is a peculiarity of the English language that we can only use the term *faith* as a *noun*. This means that we find it natural to say of a person that he or she "has faith" or does not "have faith." In this way, faith almost inadvertently comes to be thought of as a static collection of beliefs or propositions, or, at best, an externally definable set of perspectives that a person can pick up or set down much as one might a suitcase full of valuables. Yet, even as we use that static kind of language about faith, we know we are trying to communicate something more. We know somehow that to "have faith" is to be actively disposed *to trust in* and *to be committed to* someone or something. To "have faith" is to be related to someone or something in such a way that our heart is invested, our caring is committed, our hope is focused on the other.

Thus, as we examine the term *faith* more closely, two things begin to become clear. First, faith is not a *noun* but a *verb*. And second, faith is an irreducibly *relational* phenomenon. Faith is an active "mode-of-being-in-relation" to another or others in which we invest commitment, belief, love, risk, and hope.

We could limit our discussion of faith as a way-of-being-in-relation to this level of interpersonal relatedness and have it be a valuable exercise. For without the kind of commitment and regard that are involved in faithful relationships, human beings cannot become and maintain themselves as "selves."

Unless there are others who, by their consistency in caring for and interacting with us, provide the feedback by which we can form reliable images of ourselves, we cannot develop and maintain identity. As Martin Buber has shown us, unless there are "Thou's" who call forth and confirm our "I's," no selfhood is possible. Further, unless we are part of a community that uses language in faithful ways, the reality that is mediated by language will be distorted. Faith and faithfulness —at the interpersonal level—constitute foundational dimensions of the development of selves. [3]

But it is also the case that without a significant measure of interpersonal faithfulness—of "good faith" between persons —human associations, communities, societies, and the like are not viable. There is necessarily a covenantal, fiduciary* character to all lasting human communities. In our country, these imperatives of social faithfulness have recently been pressed upon our awareness as much by the realization of their absence or violation as by their presence. "Good faith" in the use of language, in the conduct of public and private affairs, and in the most personal of relationships has been badly eroded among us, leading to cynicism, disillusionment, and despair. Such erosion cannot long persist without leading to personal and societal disintegration.

The discussion of faith at the interpersonal and community levels, however, cannot be contained at those levels. For such faithfulness is neither given nor maintained in a vacuum. Faithfulness to other persons or to groups can scarcely be separated from faithfulness to the causes or values to which they are committed. Mutual faithfulness in the use of language bespeaks a shared commitment to *truth*. Success in my effort to communicate with you in these pages depends

*I use fiduciary, from the Latin "fides," rather than "trusting" for the implications of faithfulness and promise also expressed.

fundamentally on your tacit trust that as I use words and sentences I am trying to communicate the truth as I understand it. Should you begin to suspect me of using words deliberately to deceive you or to misinform you, you would withdraw the implicit faith you have invested in our mutual covenant to share truth. Consider some other instances of this tacit fiduciary, or faith structure so fundamental to human community. Mutual faithfulness in a marriage bespeaks a shared commitment not only to the partner but also to an ideal or covenant of marriage. To be a faithful member in the political community involves not only loyalty to one's fellow citizens as individuals, but also loyalty to the ideals of justice, peace, order, and the common good which give life to the purposes of the body politic.

The way-of-being-in-relation that is faith, we can begin to see, is at least *triadic* in form. We are not only bound to our neighbors in mutual loyalty as persons; we are also bound to them by the loyalties we share with them to causes or centers of value that are, in some sense, "beyond" us. When we meet someone new for the first several times, we try at some significant level of our "knowing" to identify the "causes" or values to which that person is loyal. To an important degree, our readiness to trust and risk a relationship depends upon recognizing that the other is involved in and loyal to causes beyond the self. More than any other thinkers I know, Josiah Royce and H. Richard Niebuhr have impressed upon us this triadic form of faith as relationship.[4]

Figure 1.2

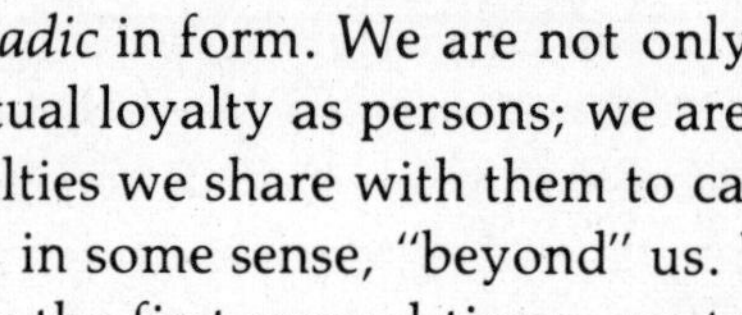

Shared Causes
or Values

Trust-in and
Loyalty-to

Self ⟷ Others

Once we have seen this triadic character of faith relatedness, pictured in Figure 2.1, we begin to recognize that the
causes or centers of value to which we give loyalty and in
which we invest trust are not objects in any ordinary sense.
Rather, they are *concepts* or *ideals* that represent orderings or
organizations of our motives and hopes, our images of
"reality," and our intuitions of coherence and purpose.

Though we must recognize the relational, interpersonal,
and triadic character of faith, we have not come to terms with
its richness and depth so long as we stay at those levels. Faith
as a way-of-being-in-relation has an outer boundary constituted by what we might call our *ultimate environment*. As
persons and communities, we live in the midst of powers,
forces, and valences that break upon us from a variety of
levels and directions. The triadic patterns of faith just discussed are part of the way we give order, coherence, and
meaning to this welter of forces and powers. But it is our tacit
and explicit assumptions about the "grain" or character of the
ultimate environment taken as a whole that provide the larger
framework of meaning in which we make and sustain our
interpersonal, institutional, and vocational covenants. It is
our operational images—conscious or unconscious—of the
character, power, and disposition of that ultimate environment toward us and our causes which give direction and
reason to our daily commitments. Faith, then, is a person's or
a community's way-of-being-in-relation to an ultimate environment. As such, it includes, permeates, and informs our
ways-of-being-in-relation to our neighbors and to the causes
and companions of our lives.

Let me illustrate: Not long ago I flew into La Guardia Air-
port on my way to give a lecture on faith development at
Fordham University. I decided to take a taxi into Manhattan
and began looking around to find someone to share the ride

and the fare. Soon I saw a casual looking but well-dressed middle-aged man. I asked him if he wanted to share a taxi. "Why not?" My companion had mastered the art of the quick opener. "What's your game?" he asked me. "I teach theology," I replied, really wanting to think about what I was going to be saying in half an hour. "Oh, you're a minister," he said. "I'm a lawyer. I practice the only kind of law you can practice and still be honest—divorce law." He rewarded my quizzical look with an explanation: "In divorces, people genuinely see things differently and they have to fight out their differences. But in all the other branches of the law, people see things the same way. They just systematically distort them in order to serve their own interests."

Then he shifted abruptly: "You people—you clergymen and theologians—you're the ones who are responsible for most of our trouble!" By now, having given up on the mental review of my speech, I decided to pick up on his challenge. "What do you mean, we are responsible for all this trouble?" "You try to convince people that they are more than animals," he said. "You try to make them believe that there is some kind of transcendent purpose to life, that there is some kind of cosmic meaning that they can be part of. It's because of this that there is so much pornography!"

I realized, of course, that I was becoming the straight man in some kind of improvised Edward Albee play, but I was curious: "All right," I said, "what sense am I to make of that? What do you mean by pornography?" "Pornography," he replied, "is the public exposure of *part* of the human being at the expense of the whole." I was impressed.

He went on to tell me that in addition to being a divorce lawyer he was an as yet unproduced playwright. He was coming to the city that day to meet with potential producers of one of his recent efforts. Hearing this, I asked him: "What assumptions do you make about your audiences? What do they come to the theater for? What do they need and want?" I thought he might share some thoughts about a philosophy of theatrical art. His quick reply was arresting: "They need and want a keyhole to look through. That's all." I asked, "But what do they want to see through the keyhole? What kind of experiences do you think they are looking for?" "Nothing in particular," he said. "They just need the keyhole."

As we neared his hotel, he said, "The way I see it, if we have any purpose on this earth, it is just to keep things going. We can stir the pot while we are here and try to keep things interesting. Beyond that everything runs down: your marriage runs down, your body runs down, your faith runs down. We can only try to make it interesting." As we parted, I told him: "I believe you have more absolutes than most religious folks I know." "I expect you're right," he said. "Have a good day."

If we take this man seriously, we must accept both the style and the content of his interchange with me as expressions of a faith outlook. In that brief taxi ride, and in that improvised "theater of the absurd" style, he shared with me some elements of a faith statement—his philosophy of life. From my standpoint as a Christian theist, his faith seems best described as negative faith, a mild nihilism. Nonetheless, his statements and style reveal the patterns by which he makes sense of an ultimate environment. And these patterns are directly linked with and seem to underlie my friend's conception of what human beings can expect of each other, of themselves, and of life.

Now let's summarize and then move ahead:

1. If we define religion primarily in its cultic and institutional sense, we must say that faith is not to be equated with religion. Faith *may be*, but is *not necessarily* "religious" in the

sense of being informed by the creeds, liturgy, ethics, and esthetics of a religious tradition. Faith, rather, is a person's or a community's way-of-being-in-relation to an ultimate environment. The character of the ultimate environment, as apprehended in faith, informs and permeates the person's or community's way-of-being-in-relation to other persons and groups, and to the values, causes, and institutions that give form and pattern to life.

2. Faith is an active or dynamic phenomenon. A verb, not a noun, faith is a way-of-being-in-relation—a stance, a way of moving into and giving form and coherence to life. But here, as we try to summarize and focus our reflections, a previously unaddressed dimension of faith must be brought into view, for who has ever seen an "ultimate environment"? As a coherent, determinate, knowable reality, it is not simply "there," in a physical sense, as is a person or an object waiting to be related to experientially and "known" through our perceptive capacities. In order to have a sense of relatedness to an ultimate environment, a person or community must *construct the idea or image of an ultimate environment.*[5] This means, then, that faith, as a mode-of-being-in-relation to the ultimate environment, involves—for individuals and communities—acts of *knowing, constructing,* or *composing* an apprehension of an ultimate environment.[6] In the effort to clarify and understand faith development, therefore, a central concern will be to focus on *how* persons or groups are *composing* or *maintaining* an apprehension of their ultimate environment, and of themselves and others as being-in-relation to it. It is time to make clear that my ecological metaphor "ultimate environment," if translated into Jewish or Christian terms, would be called "Kingdom of God," or as Teilhard de Chardin expresses it, "The Divine Milieu."

3. Finally, faith—now understood as the composing or inter-preting of an ultimate environment *and* as a way-of-being-in-relation to it—must be seen as a central aspect of a person's life orientation. Faith is a primary motivating power in the journey of the self. It plays a central role in shaping the responses a person will make in and against the force-field of his or her life. Faith, then, is a core element in one's character or personality.[9]

The Focus on Structural Development

My experience with my friend Pete in the garbage truck pro-vides a good springboard for understanding the concerns of structural developmentalists like Jean Piaget and Lawrence Kohlberg. Pete and I, as far as I can tell, were responding to the same set of perceptual stimuli. We both turned those stimuli into experiences that we could share and communi-cate. Let's review the situation: we are sitting in a black, smelly truck, traveling at 47 mph on highway #19 toward Cherokee, following a white Chevrolet. We seem to agree that the white Chevrolet is not moving farther away from us, and that we are not moving closer to the Chevrolet. Despite this apparent agreement about what we perceive and what we make of it, Pete is convinced that because the Chevrolet is in front of us on the highway it *has* to be going faster. I am equally convinced that we are proceeding at essentially the same speed.

There is a parallel between Pete's and my argument and that of a typical four-and-a-half-year-old and a typical eight-year-old about the lengths of pencils placed side by side. When the pencils are lined up end to end, both children will agree that they are the same length. When one pencil is pushed a couple of inches ahead of the other, however, the four-and-a-half-year-old will insist that the pencil that is ahead is longer. The eight-year-old, seeing the same change made, will maintain that the pencils are still equal in length: "You can push the front one back and they will still be the same," she reasons.

Pete and I, along with the two children, illustrate that different minds construct differing interpretations of the same data. This phenomenon is not news; we observe it virtually every day. What is remarkable, however, is that we are beginning to understand that our differences of interpretation are not merely random, the arbitrary functions of the content of our particular socialization experiences. Rather, they are functions of *different thought and value patterns, some of which can be systematically accounted for in developmental terms.*

Across more than fifty years of research with children and adolescents, Jean Piaget has shown us that human beings develop their mental processes in a sequence of *stages*, a sequence that is uniform from group to group and from culture to culture.[8] A stage Piaget defines as the *integrated set of mental operations* used by a person in thinking about a particular subject matter. The progression of stages over time involves *qualitative transformations* in thinking, in which new operations are integrated with, or come to supersede, older ones. Patterns of thinking develop from relatively simple, global, and undifferentiated structures to those which are successively more complex, differentiated, and comprehensive. They progress from an initial egocentric perspective through a successively augmented capacity to see and interpret things from a wide variety of possible standpoints. These stages are *hierarchical* (each successive stage carrying forward in modified and augmented form the operations of the previous stage) and *invariant* (each stage building upon the previous one so that none can be skipped). The stages and their sequence seem, on the basis of wide empirical testing, to be *universal*.[9] It should be recognized, however, that a person's or group's rate of movement through the stages and the final stage of equilibration reached are influenced by such factors as schooling, diversity of environmental stimuli, and the average cognitive level prevailing in society or sub-society. A brief overview of Piaget's stages of cognitive-structural development is given in Table 1.1.

Table 1.1
PIAGET'S ERAS AND STAGES OF LOGICAL
AND COGNITIVE DEVELOPMENT

Era I (ages 0-2) The era of sensorimotor intelligence
Stage 1. Reflex action.
Stage 2. Coordination of reflexes and sensorimotor repetition (primary circular reaction).
Stage 3. Activities to make interesting events in the environment reappear (secondary circular reaction).
Stage 4. Means-ends behavior and search for absent objects.
Stage 5. Experimental search for new means (tertiary circular reaction).
Stage 6. Use of imagery in insightful invention of new means and in recall of absent objects and events.

Era II (ages 2-5) Symbolic, intuitive, or prelogical thought
Inference is carried on through images and symbols which do not maintain logical relations or invariances with one another. "Magical thinking" in the sense of (a) confusion of apparent or imagined events with real events and objects and (b) confusion of perceptual appearances of qualitative and quantitative change with actual change.

Era III (ages 6-10) Concrete operational thought

Inferences carried on through system of classes, relations, and quantities maintaining logically invariant properties and which *refer to concrete objects.* These include such logical processes as (a) inclusion of lower order classes in higher order classes; (b) transitive seriation (recognition that if a = b and b = c, then a = c); (c) logical addition and multiplication of classes and quantities; (d) conservation of number, class membership, length, and mass under apparent change.

Substage 1. Formation of stable categorical classes.
Substage 2. Formation of quantitative and numerical relations of invariance.

Era IV (ages 11 to adulthood) Formal-operational thought

Inferences through logical operations upon propositions or "operations upon operations." Reasoning about reasoning. Construction of systems of all possible relations or implications. Hypothetico-deductive isolation of variables and testing of hypotheses.

Substage 1. Formation of the inverse of the reciprocal. Capacity to form negative classes (for example, the class of all not-crows) and to see relations as simultaneously reciprocal (for example, to understand that liquid in a U-shaped tube holds an equal level because of counterbalanced pressures).

Substage 2. Capacity to order triads of propositions or relations (for example, to understand that if Bob is taller than Joe and Joe is shorter than Dick, then Joe is the shortest of the three).

Substage 3. True formal thought. Construction of all possible combinations of relations, systematic isolation of variables, and deductive hypothesis-testing.

Piaget's inquiry has centered primarily on a person's way of constructing and reasoning about physical reality—on the apprehension of objects, space, time, causal relations, weight, mass, speed, and the like. In some ground-breaking early

SOURCE: *Lawrence Kohlberg and Carol Gilligan, "The Adolescent as a Philosopher: The Discovery of the Self in a Postconventional World,"* Daedalus *100 (Fall 1971): 1063.*

studies, however, Piaget investigated the child's use of language and symbol in play and imitation, the child's way of accounting for the origins of the visible universe, and the child's development of the capacity for moral judgment.

Inspired by this early work of Piaget's, and also by that of Plato, James Mark Baldwin, John Dewey, and others, my colleague Lawrence Kohlberg, at the Harvard Graduate School of Education, has for more than twenty years researched and written on moral development in children and adults. Kohlberg, a structural-developmentalist like Piaget, has devised a theory of moral development which shows a sequence of stages in the way people construct social or interpersonal reality.[10] His theory and research are now beginning to serve as a basis for moral education efforts in schools and prisons, and have received widespread acceptance in religious education circles. Kohlberg's stages provide a modern equivalent for the older types of "natural law" theories of ethics. Kohlberg claims that the stages of moral reasoning, in their formal or structural characteristics, are, like Piaget's stages, sequential, hierarchical, invariant, and universal. Also like Piaget, he and his associates have conducted cross-cultural research which is beginning to validate his claims. Kohlberg has appealed not only to empirical validation for his stage theory. He also argues for the ethical validity of his stages on the grounds that they are based on principles of moral reasoning that have demonstrable *universal* validity and appeal.[11] This claim means that Kohlberg's theory must be taken as a powerful challenge to the moral relativism that pervades our pluralistic world. Kohlberg's stages can be followed in Table 2.2.

Table 1.2
THE SIX MORAL STAGES

CONTENT OF STAGE	
Level and Stage	*What Is Right*
LEVEL I— PRECONVENTIONAL Stage 1—Heteronomous Morality	To avoid breaking rules backed by punishment, obedience for its own sake, and avoiding physical damage to persons and property.
Stage 2—Individualism, Instrumental Purpose, and Exchange	Following rules only when it is to someone's immediate interest; acting to meet one's own interests and needs and letting others do the same. Right is also what's fair, what's an equal exchange, a deal, an agreement.
LEVEL II—CONVENTIONAL Stage 3—Mutual Interpersonal Expectations, Relationships, and Interpersonal Conformity	Living up to what is expected by people close to you or what people generally expect of people in your role as son, brother, friend, etc. "Being good" is important and means having good motives, showing concern about others. It also means keeping mutual relationships, such as trust, loyalty, respect and gratitude.
Stage 4—Social System and Conscience	Fulfilling the actual duties to which you have agreed. Laws

Reasons for Doing Right	Social Perspective of Stage
Avoidance of punishment, and the superior power of authorities.	*Egocentric point of view.* Doesn't consider the interests of others or recognize that they differ from the actor's; doesn't relate two points of view. Actions are considered physically rather than in terms of psychological interests of others. Confusion of authority's perspective with one's own.
To serve one's own needs or interests in a world where you have to recognize that other people have their interests, too.	*Concrete individualistic perspective.* Aware that everybody has his own interest to pursue and these conflict, so that right is relative (in the concrete individualistic sense).
The need to be a good person in your own eyes and those of others. Your caring for others. Belief in the Golden Rule. Desire to maintain rules and authority which support stereotypical good behavior.	*Perspective of the individual in relationships with other individuals.* Aware of shared feelings, agreements, and expectations which take primacy over individual interests. Relates points of view through the concrete Golden Rule, putting yourself in the other guy's shoes. Does not yet consider generalized system perspective.
To keep the institution going as a whole, to avoid the break-	*Differentiates societal point of view from interpersonal agree-*

are to be upheld except in extreme cases where they conflict with other fixed social duties. Right is also contributing to society, the group, or institution.

LEVEL III—POST-CONVENTIONAL, or PRINCIPLED
Stage 5—Social Contract or Utility and Individual Rights

Being aware that people hold a variety of values and opinions, that most values and rules are relative to your group. These relative rules should usually be upheld, however, in the interest of impartiality and because they are the social contract. Some nonrelative values and rights like *life* and *liberty*, however, must be upheld in any society and regardless of majority opinion.

Stage 6—Universal Ethical Principles

Following self-chosen ethical principles. Particular laws or social agreements are usually valid because they rest on such principles. When laws violate these principles, one acts in accordance with the principle. Principles are universal principles of justice: the equality of human rights and respect for the dignity of human beings as individual persons.

---

down in the system "if everyone did it," or the imperative of conscience to meet one's defined obligations (easily confused with Stage 3 belief in rules and authority; see text).

ment or motives. Takes the point of view of the system that defines roles and rules. Considers individual relations in terms of place in the system.

A sense of obligation to law because of one's social contract to make and abide by laws for the welfare of all and for the protection of all people's rights. A feeling of contractual commitment, freely entered upon, to family, friendship, trust, and work obligations. Concern that laws and duties be based on rational calculation of overall utility, "the greatest good for the greatest number."

Prior-to-society perspective. Perspective of a rational individual aware of values and rights prior to social attachments and contracts. Integrates perspectives by formal mechanisms of agreement, contract, objective impartiality and due process. Considers moral and legal points of view; recognizes that they sometimes conflict and finds it difficult to integrate them.

The belief as a rational person in the validity of universal moral principles, and a sense of personal commitment to them.

Perspective of a moral point of view from which social arrangements derive. Perspective is that of any rational individual recognizing the nature of morality or the fact that persons are ends in themselves and must be treated as such.

SOURCE: *Thomas Lickona, ed.,* Moral Development and Behavior: Theory, Research, and Social Issues (*New York: Holt, Rinehart and Winston, 1976*), pp. 34-35.

The Structural-Developmental Approach to Faith

Piaget and Kohlberg and their followers have given us a new perspective on human thought, valuing, and behavior. They have challenged us to see that it is not just the *contents* of our ideas and values that differ; at various stages in our development the fundamental *patterns of operation* within our minds may be quite different. The child of five, in this perspective, is not just a dumb or an inexperienced adult. Rather, he or she has not yet developed certain capacities for reasoning, judging, or interpreting "reality" that will quite naturally be available at age fifteen. Put positively, the child's thinking has its own structures. These differ qualitatively from adult structures but are nonetheless coherent and integrated.

To take the example of my argument with Pete, the differences of interpretation here make sense if we understand the kind of "error" Pete had fallen into. When he assumed that because the car was in front of us it necessarily had to be going faster, he made the same error commonly exhibited by children who, according to Piaget, are in the preoperational stage of cognitive development. Pete's thinking and reasoning were dominated by only one element in his perception. He was unable to perceive the relationship between two key factors. This is not to say that Pete was unintelligent; nor are we saying that his thinking, in general, was characteristically preoperational. In this particular instance, however, Pete's logic showed the strengths, and the weaknesses, characteristic of preoperational thought.

One way to understand what we mean by "structures" of thinking and valuing is to think of the operational rules or laws which the mind follows in reasoning or making judgments. These are not conscious; we are not aware of them in such a way that we could articulate them or explain them. Rather, *they are the implicit rules underlying consciousness.* They are the patterned processes that constitute our thought.

When I became aware of the research and theories of Piaget and Kohlberg, I began to sense that the broadly phenomenological understanding of faith I had learned from Paul Tillich, H. Richard Niebuhr, and Wilfrid Cantwell Smith[12] would be susceptible to structural-developmental investigation. Why should it not be possible to examine the "testimony" of persons of faith in order to discover the implicit rules or laws governing their way of giving coherence to an ultimate environment? Why should it not be possible to uncover the patterns of valuing and interpretation underlying an individual's or group's faith outlook? As mentioned earlier, I had already devised a rough outline of religious development in order to organize the insights gathered from the life-stories heard at Interpreter's House. Erikson's theory of psychosocial development had been deeply influential in that construction, and Jung's individuation theory had made some impression on me.[13] Robert Bellah's seminal chapter on religious evolution was in my mind as a powerful structural-developmental model which could be applied at the social-cultural level.[14] This combination of experiences, reflections, and theoretical leads gave me confidence in the possibility of identifying a formally definable sequence of stages in faith development. The structural-developmental focus on thought and valuing as patterned processes, rather than as ideational content, suggested a way of making genuine comparisons across religious group lines. And the broad phenomenological-functional approach to faith on which I was working made it possible to include in these comparisons people who were not religious in any cultic or institutional sense.

In 1972-73, my associates and I began to conduct interviews designed to give us access to faith as a patterned process of thinking and valuing. Since that time, we have interviewed more than three hundred persons ranging in age from four to eighty-four. Our sample has been closely balanced between males and females and has included Catholics, Protestants, Jews, a few adherents of Eastern traditions, and a good representation of nonbelievers. The sample reflects ethnic and racial diversity, and we have sought to make it representative in regard to social class and educational background.[15] We have not conducted cross-cultural research, however, and we are only beginning the follow-up interviews with our original subjects in order to gain a longitudinal perspective. For these reasons, the stage descriptions offered here must be taken as provisional and as subject to constant refinement.

As will become apparent in my presentation of the stages, my structural-developmental approach owes much to Piaget and Kohlberg. I agree with them in regarding a stage as a structural whole of integrated operations of thought and valuing that is available to a person at a given time. Like them, I claim that stages in faith development are hierarchical, sequential, and invariant. Because of the lack of cross-cultural and longitudinal data thus far, however, it would be premature to claim universality for our stages. Also in line with Piaget and Kohlberg is my understanding of faith development as the result of an individual's *interaction* with his or her environment.†

Having suggested some of the ways in which my faith development theory is similar to cognitive and moral development theories, let me indicate one important way in which it differs. Piaget makes a rigorous distinction between *cognition* (the "structures" of knowing) and *affection* (the "energetics,"

---

†*In behaviorist or social-learning theories, growth is largely a function of the environment's influence on a passive or neutral person. In theories derived from psychoanalytic sources, development is primarily understood as resulting from biological maturation, which unfolds according to innate patterns. Theories like Piaget's and Kohlberg's stress the interplay between an active, structuring self and an equally dynamic environment.*

or motive-force, of knowing). Kohlberg tends theoretically to follow Piaget in maintaining this distinction between reason and emotion, but makes it clear that in reality the two interpenetrate and are inseparable. Both men claim, however, that cognitive structures tend to dominate the affective dynamics and that only the cognitive structures can serve as a basis for describing the sequence of developmental stages. The rationalism of Descartes and formalism of Kant stand behind this approach.

Our work, on the other hand, is significantly indebted to the psychoanalytic and depth-psychology approaches used by Erikson and Jung. These recognize the influence on rationality of unconscious dynamics, and emphasize the role of symbolic functioning in the processes of personal development and transformation. Similarly, I am indebted to theological and philosophical traditions in which knowing and valuing are held to be inseparable, and in which *will* and *reason* are seen as serving a person's dominant affections or loves. Thus, I cannot adopt the Piagetian theoretical separation of cognition and affection, of reason and emotion, but rather must account for their interpenetration in the dynamics of faith. Faith, as we are studying it, then, is a structured set of operations in which cognition and affection are inextricably bound together. In faith, the "rational" and the "passional" are fused.

Two final points before turning to the stages of faith development: First, it is necessary to keep in mind that the descriptions of stages to be given here are "still shots," and, as such, constitute interruptions of a complex and dynamic process. A look at these stages may create the impression of a staircase to be climbed on which the "climber" remains relatively unchanged or unaffected. However, the transition from one stage to another, far from representing a simple change of mind or a conscious movement from one step to another, can be a long and painfully dislocating process of relinquishment and reconstruction. Stage transition is as common as stage equilibration in a society as complex and dynamic as ours. Stage transition means enduring the dissolution of a total way of making sense of things. It means relinquishing a sense of coherence in one's near and ultimate environment. It frequently entails living with fundamental ambiguity and with a deep sense of alienation for considerable periods. In the light of this, it is understandable why we defend, shore up, and cling to our constructions of the ultimate environment, even when these prove constricting, self-destructive, or distorted.

Second, it is a serious mistake to think of these stages as constituting an achievement scale according to which we can build an accelerator-educational program. Nor should we view them as an evaluative scale by which to establish the comparative worth of persons. We have already pointed out the provisional status of the theory. Beyond that, we must emphasize that the process of "staging" a person should not be approached with a cubbyhole mentality. The stages are not boxes into which people can be stuffed. Rather, they are models by which certain interrelated patterns of our thinking, valuing, and acting may be better understood. Broadly speaking, the sequence of stages, as they are refined and validated progressively, should help clarify the aims of education and religious socialization, and should be useful in the tasks of both spiritual and psychological counseling, as well as in parenting. But development takes time. *Even* with the help of sponsoring persons,‡ institutions, or ideologies,

---

‡*"Sponsor" is a term I have taken over from Erik Erikson. A sponsor is one who stands beside, or walks with, us in development. The sponsor confirms our worth and expresses confidence in our potential. A sponsor will also confront and challenge us as well as propose (or exemplify) models by which we can develop.*

development will remain primarily the constructive task of the self in interaction with other individuals, groups, ideologies, and within the life experiences one has chosen or is given.

The Stages: Descriptions and Illustrations

My goal here is to give you an image and a feel for each of the six stages we have identified in our research. For each stage, I will provide a brief formal description of its structural characteristics. Then I will quote from one or more of our interviews with persons best described by a given stage. The quotes are offered so as to give some flesh and blood to the formal structural descriptions. Please keep in mind that it is the *structural characteristics*, not the *content*, that determines the stage of faith. For each of the illustrative interviews chosen, I could have selected from a number of others, the content and ideas of which would have been strikingly different.

In the brief formal description of each stage, I will follow a systematic format which will facilitate comparisons. Chart 2.1* presents an overview of the structural characteristics of each stage, and serves as the outline for my descriptions. Here it is necessary to indicate briefly the focus of each of the vertical columns or categories on the chart. These may best be thought of as aspects of the structural whole of a given stage.

Column A, the "Form of Logic," builds upon Piaget's theory of cognitive development. Its focus is on the patterns of judgment and reasoning available to a person at each developmental stage. The cognitive operations of each Piagetian stage are *necessary* but not *sufficient* for the corre-lated operations of each of the other columns. For this reason,

*See pages 96-99. Ed.

one can say that this theory has a cognitive-developmental focus at its core. This is not to claim that cognitive operations are paramount in our understanding of human faith. It simply indicates that we have not found the other structural characteristics of a given faith stage in the absence of the correlated level of cognitive development. Readers familiar with Piaget's work will note that we have offered substages in adulthood for his stages of formal operations. These describe different stage-typical patterns in the employment of formal operational thought in the construction of a world view, and we believe that they constitute important areas for further research.

Column B, the "Form of World-Coherence," represents a sequence of stage-typical approaches employed by persons to conceive or represent patterns of coherence in their ultimate environment. In the strand of development described, one finds some important clues for grasping the strengths and limits of each stage.

Column C, "Role-Taking," owes most to the important research on social perspective-taking conducted by Dr. Robert Selman of the Harvard Graduate School of Education.[16] Up through Stage 3 we rely explicitly on Selman's account of the development of the ability to take the perspective of others. Beyond Stage 3 we have found it necessary to extend Selman's work, to apply it to people's ability to take the perspectives of their own group, and then of groups, classes, or traditions beyond their own.

Column D, the "Locus of Authority," describes the way persons at each stage interpret and rely upon sources of authoritative insight or "truth" regarding the nature of the ultimate environment. It suggests the operational criteria characteristically employed—consciously or unconsciously—at each stage for discerning reliable authority and for choosing among competing sources.

Column E, the "Bounds of Social Awareness," focuses on how wide and inclusive the primary identifications are by which a person determines his or her community of faith. It tries to illumine both the extent and the quality of the way one takes account of and gives moral weight to the existence and claims of other individuals and groups.

Column F, the "Form of Moral Judgment," is, of course, a modification of Kohlberg's stages of moral development. The inclusion of his stages here, and their placement in the larger stage sets, indicate the correlations we are finding between his sequence of stages and ours.

Column G, the "Role of Symbols," describes a developmental sequence of levels in symbolic competence. Faith, as the composing of an ultimate environment, involves people in relations with realities that can only be represented symbolically. An important feature, therefore, of the structural whole that is a faith stage is the person's characteristic way of using or responding to symbols, rituals, myths, or metaphors.

Now we turn to the sequence of stages. To avoid repeating column names, in each stage discussion I will simply use the letter that applies from A through G. You will find a symbol at the beginning of each stage discussion that will suggest the pattern and dynamics characteristic of that stage.

Stage 1:
Intuitive-Projective

In the children we interviewed, the typical ages for Stage 1 ranged from four to seven or eight. The Stage 1 child experiences the world as fluid and full of novelty. There is a rudimentary awareness of the self as a center of experience and as the object of others' interests and concerns. Continually, the child encounters objects, situations, events, and persons of which he/she has had no previous experience and for which there are no existing inner structures for sorting and understanding.

A. Stage 1 employs *preoperational reasoning and judgment.* The child as yet lacks inductive and deductive logic; there is not yet the ability to reverse a sequence of thoughts to check reliability. As a result, causal relations are poorly understood, and their explanations of cause and effect tend to describe merely what the child perceives to have occurred. As suggested earlier, the preoperational mind tends to focus on only one dimension or feature of a situation at a time, which leads to erroneous or partial interpretations. These characteristics make the separation of fact and fantasy difficult for the child and account for the overall magical character of much of his/her thinking.

B. This undeveloped understanding of causal and temporal relationships gives to the child's construction of experience an *episodic* quality. It is as though life were a series of vivid tableaus, each interesting and complete in itself, but having no necessary relation to earlier or later tableaus. I sometimes say, jokingly, that it does not matter how often you take a child at this stage to the refreshment stand or rest room at a movie. He or she will in any case remember from the film only episodes and not the narrative line of the story. These considerations mean that the child's sense of coherence vis-a-vis the environment is largely derived from the *external* patterns of sameness and continuity provided by others in the context of home and play.

C. At Stage 1, the capacity for *taking the role or perspective* of others is severely limited. The child's thinking and valuing is *egocentric* in the true sense. Dwelling unreflectively in his or her own perceptual experience, the Stage 1 child is largely oblivious to the fact that others experience, feel, and push with their needs and interests in different ways. Other people are perceived as rounded surfaces. They are moving, talking, frowning, smiling, crying, competing or supporting bodies, whose inner springs and patterns of motivation remain as largely unnoticed and unexamined mysteries. For a parent to say to a child of this age: "Just think how that (action or attitude) makes Mommy feel!" is literally to ask for the exercise of a capacity the child does not as yet possess. Seeing laughter or tears, the child will respond with empathy to the mood. But it is a rudimentary empathy because of the child's limited ability to project into the position of another and thus to understand imaginatively what that person is feeling and why.

D. *Authority* at Stage 1 is primarily derived from the child's attachment to parents or parentlike adults whose guidance and teachings are amplified by the child's dependence upon them for nurturance and security, and by the knowledge of parental expectations gained through rewards and punishments. Beyond these attachment factors, the child's criteria for authority are based on qualities of physical size and power, or on external symbols, such as uniforms or command over large vehicles or machines. When asked where her father might have learned about what things were good and bad, one six-year-old answered typically, "Some lady bigger than him prob'ly told him."

E. The world of "significant others," as G. H. Mead terms them, for Stage 1 is the primal world of family or family-surrogate relations. Acquaintances and friends from beyond that world can have a significant impact upon the self-awareness and imagination of the child. But the degree of admissibility and the extent of their impact depend in large measure upon the approval of those more primally related. Unless the environment makes something special of them, such factors as racial, ethnic, religious, and class distinctions are not yet standard in the child's identification with the family group.

F. Properly speaking, the Stage 1 child's understanding of good and bad, right and wrong, are not "moral." He or she does not possess the conceptions of right, duty, and obligation which are required for a moral point of view. The goodness or badness of behavior is not yet related to the assessment of intention and will. Rather, the visible consequences of actions—and their results in terms of punishment or praise—constitute what is right or wrong. To break four glasses by accident, for Stage 1, is "worse"—and calls for more punishment—than to break one glass intentionally and in anger.

G. For Stage 1, *symbols* or *images* tend to function as identical with or as part of what they represent. Thus, to draw a picture of a person and then to deface it may produce an uneasy feeling of guilt or fear of retaliation, as though the person had really been harmed. There is a brilliantly illustrated children's book called *Where the Wild Things Are*[17] which depicts a fantastic repertoire of monsters like those that children encounter in their nightmares. It shows a boy of five or six in one of his dreams domesticating these fearsome beasts. This effort at a ritual purgation of nighttime anxieties is based on the insight that for young children the symbolic and the real are linked. A ritual triumph over the terrors can, therefore, be part of a real triumph.

Now I would like to invite you to overhear parts of a tape-recorded interview I had with a delightful four-and-one-half-year-old friend whom I will call Debbie. Her articulateness is unusual for her age. Her answers provide some frequently surprising illustrations of the Stage 1 mind at work. About ten minutes into our forty-five-minute interview I told Debbie a story about a little girl her age who got lost in the forest with her little brother. I asked her to pretend that she was the little girl, and then I asked her how she could make the little brother, who was frightened of the dark, feel not so scared. Here is our dialogue.

She: I'd say—put him—I would say, "If you're scared of the dark, bring a mask along."

I§: A mask? Why would you say "bring a mask"?

She: So—to scare the darkness away!

Piaget calls this kind of answer "romanticizing." It is an imaginative way of satisfying an adult who asks too many questions. In a few seconds, however, Debbie came much closer to revealing a central source of her own security in the frightening dark. I had asked, "What other things can make you feel not so scared in the darkness?"

She: Somebody with a fuzzy coat on.

I: Somebody with a fuzzy coat on? Like an animal?

She: No. My mamma has a fuzzy coat.

§*In the quotations from interviews given in these pages, "I" refers to "interviewer." In some cases, as in this one, the author is the interviewer. In others, the interviewers were my associates or students.*

A few minutes later I took another tack in my questioning. I asked: "Where do you think the sun came from, Debbie?"

She: The sky.

I: How did it get there?

She: I don't know.

I: How do you think it *might* have gotten there?

She: Before anyone was even born, you mean? Mm hm. God.

My probes about this new concept she had introduced into the discussion did not yield much for a time. Then I asked, "What do you think God might look like?

She: (Without hesitation) Air. You know why? (Why?) He's everywhere.

I: (A little taken aback by this four-year-old metaphysician) That makes sense.

She: But not in your hands.

I: (Puzzled) Not in your hands?

She: My mum said not in your hands.

I: What do you mean, not in your hands? You mean you can't hold God?

She: No, not in your hands. Not in your hands. And also she said, "When you love God, He's in your heart," and I love God.

I: And so God's in your heart? Mm hmm. I think that's a beautiful idea.

She: (quickly and firmly) And it is *true!* She's true!

Perplexed by my inability to understand her insistence "Not in your hands," I suggested we take a much needed break for orange juice and cookies. When we came back, I asked her, "What the worst thing a person can do?" After all our talk about having God in your heart and loving God I expected some answer relating to those sentiments. Instead, I got a blunt reminder of Stage 1's egocentrism:

She: (Without hesitation) Get a black eye. . . . That's what I —I got a black and blue mark on my eye once. . . . I hurt myself on a piano.

Only toward the end of the interview did I get the clue I needed to begin to unravel "Not in your hands." I asked, "Do you ever have dreams?"

She: Once when I put my eyes over my—and it was night, and I was in bed, I was really scared! (Her voice quality changed, sounded frightened and subdued.) And closer and closer! I had my eyes over my—my hands over my eyes.

I: And you were alone in your bed? And did you have a dream? What did you dream about?

She: That it kept on getting closer and closer and closer.

I: What is *it*—what kept getting closer and closer?

She: Something that kept on going around and around, got closer and closer to me. (Remembered terror sounded in her voice.)

I: And made you very scared? Well, what happened?

She: I started crying. (You woke up?) And started crying.

I: Where do dreams come from?

She: I don't know. (Where would you *think?*) I don't *know.*

I: If I were in the room with you, could I see the thing coming? (No.) Could anyone see it? (Only me.) Why?

She: Because. (Pause) Cause—Cause it's—cause I saw it in my hands.

I: In your hands? (Uh huh. So nobody else could see it.) Could you hold it in your hands? (No.) Well, how, how did you see it in your hands?

She: Just—put your hands over *your* eyes and see if *you* could see anything.

I: (Finally getting the picture—or at least its location!) Oh, I see what you mean; you had your hands over your eyes, and you saw it. I see. I see. Well, where was it?

She: Right next to my hand.

Whether the dream is a very thin substance right next to her hand, or a picture projected there somehow, I will never know. But because God is like the air—everywhere—perhaps that is why she insists, "Not in your hands." In another place when asked if God is a person she had said, "He can see us, but we can't see Him." And then *she* asked, "How come?"

Like all our Stage 1 respondents, Debbie's thoughts and feelings about the character of her ultimate environment are a collage of images and beliefs she has been given by trusted others, mixed with her own experiences and fanciful, imaginative constructions. Our interviews with older persons and our biographical studies of outstanding religious and cultural leaders alert us to the fact that these intuitive-projective constructions, and the deep sentiments both of love and dread that are attached to them, frequently constitute a powerful bedrock of conviction on which later, more adult forms of faith may be grounded.

Stage 2: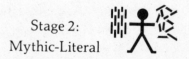
Mythic-Literal

The typical age range for Stage 2 in our sample was from six or seven to eleven or twelve. In a number of instances, we also found adolescents and adults whose world-views dominantly exhibited the structural patterns of this stage. This reminds us that in structural-developmental theories, stage level is not necessarily tied to chronological age or to biological maturation. Exceptions aside, in our society, Stage 2 is found most often in middle to late childhood. The transition from Stage 1 may occur over the space of a year or two, and, typically, by age eleven or twelve, a gradual transition to Stage 3 is under way. As the left-hand part of the picture may suggest, the world of Stage 2 is more linear and orderly than that of Stage 1. In the world of perceptual experience, the boy or girl typically becomes a young empiricist, separating the real from the unreal on the basis of practical experience. Alongside this now more orderly empirical world, however, there is usually a very private world of speculative fantasy and wonder. This is a world of hope and terror; of reassuring images and myths in daydreams; of undermining fears in nightmares and waking consciousness.

A. Cognitively the child has acquired *concrete operations.* Though still subject to errors and omissions, he or she can now mentally review a sequence of observed actions and deduce causal relationships. Thinking is now reversible. Observing a set of similar patterns of action, the child can now form by induction a generalized principle or rule that will account for and make possible the prediction of those patterns under other circumstances. The child at Stage 2 spontaneously generates and uses categories and classes based on the physical characteristics of objects, and can include subclasses under more general headings. In these ways, concrete operations bring about the gradual freeing of thought and reasoning from the domination of perception and feeling. But thought remains tied to the concrete world of sensory experience and does not yet make extensive use of abstract concepts.

B. With the development of a new understanding of time, causality, and the conformity of action to a certain natural lawfulness, Stage 2 achieves mastery of the *narrative* mode for giving coherence to experience. Without the capacity—or the need yet—to interrupt the stream of life and reflect more abstractly upon its meaning or direction, the individual best described by Stage 2 employs stories or myths, whether personal or cultural-religious, to express his or her sense of an ultimate environment.

C. Stage 2 marks a major gain in role-taking ability. Now the boy or girl spontaneously makes allowance for the fact that from another person's vantage point an object he or she is viewing will appear different. The skill of projecting oneself imaginatively into the position or situation of another is developing, thus making a more adequate empathy possible.

D. The claims of authorities, insofar as they relate to areas of the boy's or girl's sensory experience, will be subjected to the child's own forming canons of judgment in that area. But in other areas, and for the validation of conclusions drawn from their own experience, children look to trusted adults—teachers or parents—or to older siblings. The question of authority is not a conscious issue at Stage 2. Choices are made and preferences are expressed and relied upon, but the criteria by which these are made are not yet matters of conscious reflection.

E. The bounds of the social world have widened in Stage 2. The family matrix has been concentrically supplemented by relationships with teachers and other school authorities, with friends and their families, perhaps with leaders or other participants in a religious group, and by encounters with street life, television, movies, or reading. In this stage, typically, such characteristics as the family's ethnic or racial heritage, religious affiliation, and social class standing have become important aspects of the child's self-image. Identifications are strong with "those like us," while the images of "those who are different" can be harshly stereotypical. *

F. Due largely to the advance in role-taking abilities, the form of moral judgment in Stage 2 has a new element of reciprocity and a new conception of fairness. Though they have not yet developed a system of reciprocal rights and duties, Stage 2 children do take account of the needs and demands of others in the pursuit of their own aims and goals. Likewise, they expect others to make allowances for their demands. Kohlberg calls the form of moral judgment at this stage "instrumental hedonism," and to suggest the concrete level of reciprocity, he frequently subtitles it: "You scratch my back, and I'll scratch yours."

G. The identification of symbol and symbolized that distinguished Stage 1 gives way in Stage 2 to a kind of *literal-correspondence* understanding. For Stage 2, a symbol must refer to something specific. Though this may be an imaginative idea or concept, Stage 2 will typically imagine it by analogy with some element of concrete experience. We were surprised at the lack of anthropomorphic imagery in the representations of God at Stage 1. But at Stage 2, among those children whose nurturing environments have made a place for meaningful reference to God, the most favored images or symbols for God are anthropomorphic. This correspondence approach to symbolism, and the tendency to

---

*But there is also a dangerous reverse possibility here. Where the child comes to view some or all of the characteristics of his own family or group as inferior in these respects, there can be a powerfully destructive transformation of valuing in which the stereotyped images of "those different from us" are given an excessive positive evaluation, and one's own group identity is unduly negativized.

use concrete analogies, further explain why dramatic narrative and myth are Stage 2's favored modes for constructing and communicating a sense of transcendent meaning.

To illustrate some typical Stage 2 responses, I want to share a few passages from two interviews. The first is with a boy of eight, whose responses indicate an early phase of Stage 2 with some strong vestiges of Stage 1. The second is with a boy of ten and a half who is beginning a transition to Stage 3. Both boys are unusually articulate. Our eight-year-old I will call Will. Early in our interview I asked Will, "What do you think children of your age might be most worried about?"

He: Their mother or their father.

I: Afraid that something might happen to them?

He: Yes, like if, like, I didn't know what happened to my uncle. I mean I really got worried. I forgot about it a few minutes and then I remembered. (Voice becomes plaintive and sad.) Oh no, I don't want him to die. No. I went upstairs and I said a prayer and then came back. My mom was looking down at the floor and I said, "Is he OK?" and she said, "He's dead." So I started to cry.

To relieve the strain of this obviously fresh account of grief —he came back to this recent death three times in the interview—I asked him whether the uncle was his mother's or his father's brother. In relief, he launched into an impressive demonstration of concrete operational virtuosity in classification:

He: I know what my mother, my mother's, wife is, I mean my mother's mother is. I know who my father's mother is and my father's father and my mother's mother. But my mother's mother died. My mother's *father* died. I'm getting mixed up with my mother's father and my mother's mother and my father's father and my father's mother.

Somewhat further on I asked him, "What happens to people when they die?" (We had talked about ghosts earlier in a playful way, and then he had described his uncle's death. I expected something thoughtful on this topic.)

He: Oh, they get pale. They have white all over them. Like, my brother read this story—and he was about to attack a bear. And the bear attacked him and he didn't know it but his face was literary, literally torn off. . . . There was just pale hanging down. . . .

Will's penchant for telling dramatic stories came to the fore again when I asked him how the first people came to be on the earth.

He: All right. The first people on earth were Adam and Eve. The way they got there was by God. They made them. And God gave them a special place, some garden, I forget the name of it, and Adam [sic] saw a garden snake, so she heard it and he said, "Take this apple, then eat it." So she took it, she took a bite of it, it was good and so she ate it, then she went to Adam and said, "Hey Adam, this is good. Why don't you take a bite?" So he took a bite and then God came down and said, "You have took a bite." God said, "You can't eat from that tree," and they heard him but they didn't listen, so God punished them. He told an angel to go down and guard the garden, they couldn't go back to the garden and that was their home, so they couldn't go back into it. And the angel was standing guard with a flame of fire, you know, on the other side of the garden there was another

angel with a burning knife. They had to go find some-
where else to live.

Will drew on more of his catechetical training when I
asked, near the end of the interview, "Could you explain to
someone what you understand about God?"

He: OK. Well, if you want to know who God is, I don't
know. He could be a spider, he could be anything, even
a snake. But, God is our father, he's supposed to be a
man. Mary is our mother. God is in*vin*cible. And there,
there, there's like another person, there's three people
that are part God, mostly God. The Holy Spirit, Jesus
and God. . . .

I: Does God talk to people?

He: When they're dead, yes.

I: But not when they are alive?

He: Yes, well, in a way, yeah. When you pray.

I: Does God cause things to happen?

He: No. Well, yes. He causes people to love one another. He
helps. And he causes—I don't know how he does it—
but he causes the devil to have pain somehow. He
makes it rain and there's only one way it can rain—(a
bit smugly) *by God's power.* And if God wasn't looking
at you right now, or taking care of you, you wouldn't
be alive.

I: God makes the decision about when we should die?

He: Yes. He calls you up there. He calls you up to heaven,
yes.

In the latter part of this passage, we seem to be getting
Will's own ideas. When I asked him this last question, he
spoke with obvious feeling:

I: Are you afraid of dying?

He: Well, I've been wanting to die to see my uncle, but then I've thought about it. No, I don't want to die, I like it the way it is. But if God's up there, I don't care. I'd rather go up there.

Will's answers, with their extremely literal quality and close reliance upon what he had been taught, may in three years be more like those of eleven-year-old Stan, who, though still largely confined to the concreteness and narrative qualities of Stage 2, has imaginatively pressed them to their limits and beyond. After he had speculated about the existence of UFOs, telling about a couple of stories he had read, I asked Stan: "If there were creatures on other planets in the universe, do you suppose they'd be hostile, or do you suppose they would be friendly?"

He: Well, some could be hostile, some could be friendly. I just—there's just one thing I have always believed in. (What's that?) It's impossible that we're the only people around, because, you know, space just goes on and on. We don't know how far and it just seems impossible that life is only on one planet.

I: How do you think life originated?

He: From the sea, but I don't know how that came about. In science books it's from the sea, but in the Bible God made Adam and Eve and all the animals, but . . . mostly the Bible tells *why*, and science tells *how*. So I just kind of go by that. . . .

I: Is there any conflict between the Bible story and . . .?

He: Well, they say, "Adam and Eve," and "seven days," but we don't know that it wasn't three million years, you know, or sixty million years before we came around. It just could have been that days were half a million years or something, you know.

Stan's empiricism and his precocious skill at reconciling the Biblical and scientific standpoints are both vividly called into play as this exchange continued.

I: Would you say that both the Bible account and science are true, or is one more true than the other?

He: Well, I think they both are. Maybe there's some places in the Bible where somebody put down something they thought they saw, like Jesus rising up off the mountain. It could have just been that the disciples had been so excited and so sorry at the same time at seeing him go for the last time, that they just imagined him rising up above their heads. Nobody knows if that's true or if some of the things in the Bible are true, like how one guy lived three hundred years. It could have just been that he lived eighty years except they measured years different then. Maybe six months was ten years. You'd have to do some mathematical problems to figure it out exactly. . . .

A recurrent theme in Stan's interview was an almost despairing awareness of the ecological damage caused by human technology and warfare. The other side of this concern was a strong romantic conception of the balance of nature and animal life within it before the emergence of humans. Responding to these consistent emphases, I asked, "Do you think it was a colossal mistake, then, that human beings ever appeared on the scene?"

He: No. Because at first we weren't doing anything against nature. We were living with them or at least in the Bible we were, or in science as monkeys, we were nature. But then as we started evolving and then we turned into Homo sapiens, what we are now. Our brains are destroying us. We are so smart and we are building so much that it's going to kill us all. Like the automobiles we're making, they're just pouring out poison.

I: Well, are you saying, then, that human beings are somehow basically flawed or have something wrong with them, or did they change from the time of the Bible until now?

He: They have, yes, because back then we built smaller houses and small cities and didn't make them real high. We didn't have cars to pollute the air. The only thing we were doing then was raising dust and breathing out. But the dust would settle with the rain and the carbon dioxide would go into the plants and they'd put out oxygen. We might have had some evil then, like, people got killed. And people kill each other now, and that's just not right, but—Adam and Eve were perfect, almost, until they ate the apple—I'll put it that way.

I: What did that mean, when they ate the apple?

He: That started the evil that just spread. There is not a place in this world there's no evil, except animals. They don't know, you know, what they're doing, you know, the killing. They just know they've got to eat.

The eating of the apple became a sort of bottom line in every analysis Stan offered of man's inhumanity to man and to animals. Eventually, he spontaneously shared his version of the Adam and Eve story. Then, in the midst of a projection of future conditions in 1994, which included a discussion of jet-powered air cars, Stan returned to the myth of the fall:

He: But I just don't think we will ever find anything that we won't need gasoline for. A long time ago we didn't even know that it was here. We didn't try to process it. We didn't need it because—if God had just told them not to eat the tree, and then they'd taken off all the fruit or something, I don't think this would have come about because there was no other way for evil to come around except for the devil.

I: Tell me a little about the devil in that story. Do you believe the devil is a—well, what do you believe about the devil?

He: The devil is just a—emotions of people made physical into a mythical character. It's—what the devil is is evil, and he might have taken the form of a snake, but all he was, was evil in the form of a snake. That's what the devil is, evil. Because, if you take the "d" off of it, it is evil, and like that, somebody just took evil and put something on it, and made the word, devil.

I: Is that something somebody told you, or is that something you figured out for yourself?

He: That's what I think. That's just what I think.

I: Now, when you say the devil is a "mythical character," what does that mean?

He: It means that people think that he is physical, that he is bodily, but he is in our bodies. But he does not have a body; he uses ours to do what he wants.

I: Well now, how would you talk about God? Is God a mythical character too?

He: He is physically; so is the devil, physically, but they are both here in our thoughts and minds. They just—and I just—I don't see why we came around. How did God take the trouble to make us? He didn't have to. He could have just left us monkeys, with no evil or anything—just monkeys.

Stan's overwhelming awareness of "evil" and disillusionment with the human species are not atypical in observant, thoughtful boys and girls his age. These sensibilities, combined with a concrete operational inability to imagine the

finality of personal death, may be part of the explanation for
the alarming increase in suicides by children of ten and
eleven. It is as though they have taken on a precocious responsibility for a disastrous future and past, the conceiving of
which overwhelms their capacities for reflective transcendence. In Stan's case, the interview ended with a spontaneous
sharing of an esthetic delight which both disclosed a source of
strength for him and gave him one last coda on his central
theme.

I: How do you go about judging whether or not you'd
        trust someone enough to talk about important things
        with him?

He: I don't know. Somehow it just happens. There's just one
        thing that I just thought of that I've always thought is
        good about humans. Music—I love music, any kind.
        But, I've heard on, like . . . My brother, my small
        brother, he's not even two yet and he likes to watch
        Sesame Street because of Big Bird and all these. Some-
        times I have to keep him, so I just watch it with him.
        There's one part they put on it maybe once a week or
        something, and it's accompanied by music. There's just
        no words. There don't have to be. And it proves a
        point that I've been talking about. It shows parts of a
        flower just going up from the bottom up to the top. And
        it's just pretty and it goes—um-um—I can't remember
        how it goes, but it's just beautiful music, played on a
        piano, I believe. And then when it shows the top of the
        flowering parts, all it is is just a wind, but it's so pretty
        —the flower part. And then it goes up, it goes away
        from the flower and it shows how it's just on a small
        clump of ground with just a few weeds around it, on a
        big high brick building. And it goes out to the side and it
        shows the Brooklyn Bridge—it's in Brooklyn—and it's

just ugly, just to see what it is. You can't see very far,
and it's just so black, it's just so heavy smog, and it's all
man-made. And then you see that flower. . . .

Stage 3:
Synthetic-Conventional

Stage 3 has both adolescent and adult versions. We do not
find the transition from Stage 2 to 3 before ages eleven or
twelve. Some persons may begin the transition out of Stage 3
as early as ages seventeen or eighteen. But for many, it comes
later, and a significant number of adults are best described by
Stage 3 right through middle age and into their older adulthood.

A hallmark of Stage 3 is its way of structuring the world
and the ultimate environment in interpersonal terms. One of
the great gains that comes with the application of early formal
operational thinking to social relationships is the ability to
perform what Selman has taught us to call mutual role-
taking. In mutual role-taking, the individual constructs an
image of the self as seen by others, and simultaneously takes
account of the fact that other persons are performing the same
operations in their relationships. This operative awareness of
mutual role-taking results in a kind of "third person" perspective on the relationship with other persons, with events and
objects, or with what we might call "the world."

This revolutionary set of sensitivities—not available, even
to bright and precocious youngsters like Stan, at Stage 2—
results in people becoming temporarily or permanently dependent upon "significant others" for the construction and

maintenance of their sense of identity, and for sanctioning the beliefs, values, and action guidelines by which they shape a way of moving into and taking hold of life. Stage 3 is a "conformist" stage in the sense that it is acutely tuned to the expectations and judgments of others, and as yet does not have a sure enough grasp on its own identity or faith in its own judgment to construct and maintain an independent perspective. But as the picture representing Stage 3 suggests, conformity is no simple or easy matter. For the person at Stage 3—whether adolescent or adult—life is segmented into related and overlapping "theaters" of action and relation. These "theaters" may include family or other intimate groups, work or school, politics, peers, leisure, fantasy, public life, the media, and perhaps religion. In each of these theaters, there are both individual and collective, or group, significant others. These expectations, evaluations, and judgments count heavily for the person. But across these theaters, the significant others are not always in agreement. Faith and identity at Stage 3 must therefore find a way of synthesizing these valued expectations and judgments. For both adolescents and adults, this usually means adopting one of the two possible strategies: On the one hand, one can *compartmentalize,* "When with my peers, I will do as they expect; when with my parents, I will comply with their wishes." On the other hand, one can create a *hierarchy* of authorities, whereby peers and their values become most important, with other "authorities" being subordinated to them. For adults best described by Stage 3, these patterns have become so habituated that such persons often appear quite individuated and autonomous. A careful, probing interview, however, will reveal that the significant others and their expectations, which were formative in another period and in other contexts, are still carried "within" as the reference points by which beliefs, values, and actions are validated and sanctioned.

Now let us return to our familiar format of explicating the chart.

A. *Cognitively*, Stage 3 requires at least *early formal operations*. This means that it requires a standpoint once removed from the concrete data of experience and from the activities of classification, seriation, and of deductive and inductive reasoning that are characteristic of concrete operational thought. It involves being able to construct classes of classes and the ability to imagine hypothetical possibilities of action and interpretation that extend beyond concrete experience. It involves beginning to think about one's thinking, and to evaluate one's valuing, at least at the intermediate level of seeing one's thoughts, values, and actions from the imaginatively constructed viewpoint of significant others.

B. The *coherence of one's experience of the world* at Stage 3 is synthetic in a predialectical sense. The ideas, beliefs, and values one espouses as a result of interaction and mutual role-taking with significant individual and collective others are melded into a tacit (not critically self-aware) system. The person best described by Stage 3 *has* deeply felt beliefs and values, acts on them, and defends them. But, typically, he or she grounds such beliefs and values on the authority of a significant other or a valued group consensus, whose authority is taken to be self-evidently valid. The tacitness of the system is further manifested in the frequently contradictory values and beliefs it contains, in the often vague and undifferentiated conceptual quality of the values and beliefs, and in the person's readiness to live with a wide "penumbra of mystery" (as H. L. A. Hart puts it) surrounding his or her central affirmations and their validations.

C. *Role-taking* at Stage 3 is mutual and leads to a "third person" perspective that is essential to self or mind. The leap forward constituted by the awareness of others' judgments and expectations helps account for Stage 3's deep concern about "what *they* will think" and for its heavy reliance upon interpersonal virtues, such as sincerity, loyalty, genuineness, self-assurance, or charisma, as criteria for evaluating the truth or value of the perspectives people represent.

D. *Authority* for Stage 3 is constituted by trust-evoking personal qualities in potential leaders or the representatives of ideas or movements. Also, the appearance of sanction by legitimating social institutions is often important. To be credible, a spokesperson must usually "look the part," possess a conventionally** expected style and mannerisms, have the approval of some personally valued institution or institution-like group, and come across as sincere, genuine, and truthful.

E. The interpersonal construction of experience comes sharply into focus in Stage 3's *bounds of social awareness*. One's own identity and faith are derived from membership in a group or groups characterized primarily by face-to-face relationships. In this context, "group" may be defined by any one or some combination of the following: ethnic-familial ties, social-class norms, regional perspectives and loyalties, religious system, technoscientific ethos, peer values and pressures, and sex role stereotypes. Individual members of outgroups may be related to as *persons* and be appreciated for their individual virtues and qualities. "Some of my best

---

#In third person perspective-taking, I see you seeing me; and I see you seeing me seeing you. The coordination of these multiple perspectives enables one to see self-other interactions with a revolutionary new kind of objectivity.

**Remember that conventional *is a very relative term. There are conventional "leftists" and conventional "rightists," conventional counterculture and conventional traditional-culture orientations. The key is the degree of conformity involved.*

friends are _____s." But out-groups as groups—and the experiences, values, beliefs, and styles that characterize them —are likely to be understood in stereotypical and prejudicial terms.

F. *Moral judgment* at Stage 3, in keeping with the interpersonal focus of the stage as a whole, is based on fulfilling the expectations of significant others and maintaining agreement or peace between persons. This, of course, is Kohlberg's Stage 3. It is often the case, however, that persons of Stage 3, particularly adults, also exhibit the structuring capacities that approximate Kohlberg's later conventional stage, the Stage 4 "Law and Order" orientation. This latter pattern, which correlates Stage 3 faith and Stage 4 moral judgment levels, is more frequently found in the men in our sample. Stage 3 faith correlated with Stage 3 moral judgment level is more frequently found in women.††

G. In Stage 3, *symbols* no longer have the literal-correspondence quality found in Stage 2. The individual of Stage 3 understands metaphor and double entendres and is prepared to allow symbols to affect him or her at a variety of levels simultaneously. There is typically a precritical or "naive"[18] apprehension of the symbol. Yet in a more complex way than at Stage 2, the symbol and the symbolized are bound together in a natural or primal linkage. The symbol and the symbolized are naturally or necessarily correlated. Typical images of God at Stage 3 are no longer physically anthropomorphic, but are based on "personal" qualities of the deity—for instance, God as friend, companion, "lifeline," comforter, guide, "mind."

---

††*In a larger book now in preparation, I intend to discuss this point and some possible explanations for it in greater detail.*

Of the many examples of Stage 3 patterns of faith outlook from which we could choose, let's consider parts of an interview with a Catholic wife and mother in her early thirties.

Let's call her Mrs. M. The interviewer began by asking a very general question: "What is the purpose of human life?" Our respondent floundered a bit (as any of us would) in coming to terms with the question, then replied:

She: People are for people. In order to have life, you have to have life around you. People are important to other people . . . just the companionship. . . . It's just love. When you stop and think, to have another person to love, to know you can love them back . . . just to be wanted.

I: Perhaps you could speak for yourself: How do you think about the purpose of *your* life, your *own* reason for being?

She: You know, that's a really tough question: what is the purpose of life? I can't remember just stopping to think of it. . . . Right now, the purpose of my life is my family; my family that I have, my family that I came from. I have no other goal. I don't want to be a famous writer or painter, I'm happy from day to day. I consider myself a kind of happy person. Happy at what I'm doing—I know that's what I should be doing 'cause I'm so happy doing it . . . I feel fulfilled at the end of the day. I don't feel, "Oh, gee, what am I going to do tomorrow, or what a lonely day this was." I like being where I am and helping the people that are here and having them around me.

Mrs. M's expression of contentment with her life is made somewhat poignant by the next several passages in her interview. There she tells us that, from about the fifth grade in

parochial school on, she coasted along, getting by with
minimal work and minimal achievement and with people
making allowances for her because she was "good." Her sharing of this information reveals that Mrs. M had been giving
this set of factors in her life a good deal of thought:

She: In grammar school, I can remember it started in the fifth
grade, 'cause that's when there's multiplication tables
and stuff like that. It just seemed like one day I found
the class doing something different and I didn't know
what they were talking about. I wasn't paying attention
up till that point and then I lost all that. And they just
assumed I couldn't do it, and I assumed it's easier that
way, so I went along with it. I really think, after a lot of
thought, that's where it all started and since then that's
the way your life pattern goes.

The interpersonal framework of Mrs. M's outlook has already become apparent through her references to family and
family-like relationships as the focal point in her life. Later in
the interview, she was asked, "Why is it that some groups or
peoples seem to suffer more in life than others?" In a manner
characteristic of Stage 3, her answer takes little or no account
of social-structural or political factors but is again formulated
in terms of face-to-face, interpersonal models:

She: Some groups suffer. I guess if I knew why, I'd probably
be running for office or something that could really help
people out. I really think that the people that are truthful, they're poor probably. There's a lot of poor people.
But I feel if you're truthful and you're fair to yourself,
you're going to be fair to other people. You're a much
better person, you're much better off than the person
that's rolling in money and cheating on someone else,
because they're not comfortable. It's like when you tell a

lie, you have to lie again, you have to keep building on that lie. . . .

Similarly, when asked what people could do to make the world a better place, Mrs. M again drew upon thought patterns taken from models of interpersonal role-taking.

She: The world would be a better place if people would stop and listen. I'm guilty of that too. I should stop. Sometimes the world's too busy, like I'm too busy making supper and the kids come up to me and start talking and it's "Just a minute." Well, I think that's the way the world is. Everybody's just too busy to stop and listen to what the person next to him has to say. And I don't think you can get anywhere unless you stop and sit down and really listen because people have things to say.

Both the conformist character of Stage 3 and the tacit quality of the beliefs and values it espouses can be seen in Mrs. M's response to the question, "How do you as an adult determine what is right or wrong for you?"

She: Knowing what is right or wrong is just the way you feel, I guess, the way you've been brought up. You know when you're doing something wrong by the way you feel. Not that I've always been perfect or done the right thing. As far as me deciding for someone else, I couldn't do that. I'd have to decide for myself, because I know what's right for me, or just the way you feel.

Further on in the interview Mrs. M talks about her conceptions of and feelings about God as well as about her own religiousness. The quotes that follow here omit the questions of the interviewer:

She: I picture God as the religion books say, an all-knowing and loving God . . . an all-loving and all-powerful person—and a person! The religion books point that out, but that's what I *feel.* I feel God *is* powerful and he's all loving. A lot of people don't agree with the old religion books or don't like the idea, but I got something out of it. I still remember stuff from the book. I consider God like a lifeline, a friend, because during the day you're working around and I talk to him. I think, and in thinking, I talk to him. I believe there is a God and he hears what I'm saying and knows what I'm thinking and is there to help me. . . .

. . . I'm religious as far as I know how to be religious, but there's a lot of parts of my religion that I don't know about. And now things are becoming a little more complex—it's an awful thing, but I don't care! Because I feel that as long as I believe in God and I feel about God the way I do that no matter what they're teaching now, to me it's not going to make any difference. I shouldn't feel that way. I should be wanting to grow and be really interested in finding out about this [about the changes in Church teaching since Vatican II].

In these passages we see a reliance upon external authorities, an undifferentiated fusion of "feeling" and "thinking," and a readiness to live with a penumbra of mystery around her central symbols or beliefs. All these are features that typify Stage 3 as seen in adults. We also note the perplexity that arises when previously reliable authorities begin to change or to be superseded.

In some ways, it is unfair to quote selectively from an interview such as this one with Mrs. M. Without reading the whole "event," it may be hard to fully appreciate the evidences of grace and stability, of compassion, and of good-humored strength which suffuse her responses as a whole. These qualities of her faith outlook remind us forcefully that each stage is a potentially well-integrated structure for composing and maintaining a meaningful, useful life. Both the evidences of strength and some beginning signs of a restiveness and readiness for transition find expression in one of Mrs. M's concluding remarks:

She: I think if you know yourself you know God. I think I'm an extension of God. And I know what I am, but I know there should be more expected of me than what I'm doing. I should be more interested in learning. And maybe, eventually I will be, because just in this past year I've noticed a change in me and I realize that it isn't stupid to ask questions that I can ask. But I believe that if you want to really do anything, you can do anything. Consequently, if you want to really know God, you can know yourself, and then through yourself you can know God.

Stage 4:
Individuating-Reflexive

In the transition to Stage 4, the self starts to emerge from its previous encircling dependence upon significant others for the construction and maintenance of an identity and faith. The sense of self is now reciprocal with a faith outlook or worldview which mediates between the self and significant others, thus giving individuals a qualitatively different degree of autonomy. At Stage 4, there is an awareness of having a determinate outlook or faith. This person knows that his or

her own views are different from those of others. In recognizing this particular outlook or faith perspective, the person at
Stage 4 knows that his or her perspective is vulnerable to
challenge and change, and that a justification of its truth and
adequacy is therefore required. Stage 4's individual is
generally aware of the boundaries and the inner connections
of the beliefs and values that constitute the larger perspective.
People at this stage hold themselves and others accountable
for authenticity, congruence, and consistency in the relation
between self and outlook.

This ability to stand alone or apart at Stage 4, with its
qualitatively new awareness of and responsibility for an independent ideology or outlook, helps explain why we call it
the Individuative-Reflexive stage. It is a mistake, however, to
assume that it is necessarily an *individualistic* stage. A person
at Stage 4 does not necessarily separate from former face-to-
face groups, from interpersonal relations, or from a particular
social class, religious background, or institutional ties. What
does change is that those relationships—which, at Stage 3,
were essential to a derived identity and outlook—now at
Stage 4 become the *expressions* of a more autonomous
identity and outlook which have begun to shape their own
determinate forms.

Frequently the transition from Stage 3 to Stage 4 is a somewhat protracted affair. The transition may begin around ages
seventeen to eighteen, though we rarely find well-equilibrated
Stage 4 characteristics before the early twenties. It is not un-
common to interview adults at all ages who are best described
as 3-4 transitional types and who give evidence of having
been there for a number of years. For some, the transition
comes later, in the thirties or forties. When this occurs, it is
experienced as a more profound disruption, often bringing a
sense of temporary "breakup" as well as of "breakthrough."

Now let's turn again to the chart and look at the categorical descriptions for Stage 4.

A. Full *formal operations* are required for the reflection upon self, upon outlook or perspective, and upon the relationship of the latter to "reality," which characterizes Stage 4. Because of the need to establish and maintain the self's boundaries in identity and faith, the person at Stage 4 characteristically tries to differentiate himself or herself from others and to hammer out an independent perspective. This gives the Stage 4 individual a certain "either/or" quality and leads us to characterize the *style* of applying formal operations reflexively to oneself and one's outlook as "dichotomizing."

B. Because at Stage 4 a world-view or faith is constructed, and because a self-awareness of that faith's boundaries and inner connections exists, we say that the form of world coherence is that of an *explicit system.* The individual at Stage 4 typically aspires to a comprehensive ideology. In striking contrast to Stage 3, the Stage 4 person employs abstract concepts freely in the construction and communication of an outlook. These concepts do not exhibit the vague, amorphous quality of Stage 3, but are more internally differentiated. Nor are persons at Stage 4 content to live with a Stage 3 "penumbra of mystery" surrounding their central concepts, beliefs, and values.

D. Stage 4 role-taking builds upon the mutual role-taking of the previous stage. But it adds a new level of complexity. Now there is a concern to see and judge oneself and one's own outlook in the light of others' outlooks or world-views. Both in the effort to maintain the boundaries of one's own (or one's group's) world-view and in the interest of justifying one's own truth in the face of competing perspectives, Stage 4 persons typically distort their constructions of others' perspectives in unconscious ways. Conscious recognition of these subtle distortions becomes one factor indicating the limits of one's Stage 4 faith. When a new quality of accuracy and comprehensiveness begins to be achieved in this respect, the boundaries of one's own identity and perspective have to be widened and relaxed, leading to a transition to Stage 5.

D. When the Stage 4 person looks at potential authority figures or an authoritative ideological perspective, the criteria of acceptance or rejection are based on a complex comparison of "reality," as seen and experienced through his or her own outlook, with the truth or reality claims of the person or perspective in question. This means that authority for Stage 4 is validated by internal processes and that truth has an ideological or systemic quality. Truth must "fit" with other elements of one's outlook taken as a whole. We must not leave the impression, however, that the exercise of these criteria is a purely rational or intellectual operation. At Stage 4, as with all stages, we are speaking of the relation to "truth," and to the authority that mediates it, as combining intellectual and emotional dynamics, as every act of evaluation must.

E. At Stage 4 a person's reference group(s), for purposes of identification and inclusiveness in calculating moral responsibility, may be quite wide. There is at least a formal recognition of the diversity and relativity of different group interests and an implicit recognition of the obligation to take the claims and perspectives of other groups (classes, ethnic or racial groups, national communities, religious communities, and the like) into account over against one's own. But because of the psychological imperative of justifying and preserving the boundaries of one's own or one's group's perspectives, Stage 4 tends to honor *caricatures* of the perspectives of other groups, not recognizing that they are caricatures. Functionally, this means that Stage 4's *real* inclusion of the perspectives of others typically is assimilated in subtle ways to its own class or group norms and perspectives.

F. The *form of moral judgment* at Stage 4 is postconventional and may be principled at Kohlberg's Stage 5 level. Functionally, however, due to the assimilation of other groups' perspectives to one's own, a Stage 4 person's principled morality still has a class or group bias, though the animating intention is an ideal of justice. Many people at Stage 4 are not principled in regard to moral judgments. These individuals are better described as reflective relativists or "contextualists." Though beyond the law and order stage, they do not as yet have nonrelativist principles for adjudicating moral dilemmas.

G. Symbols, myths, rituals, and the like are typically found meaningful at Stage 4 if their "content" can be translated into usable concepts. In Stage 4, the way of being informed by the symbolic sphere parallels what Ricoeur calls a "reductive hermeneutic"—a more or less critical demythologization in which the import of a symbol, ritual, or myth is separated from the entity itself and is conveyed in terms of ideas or propositions. This approach to the symbolic is clearly a function of the Stage 4 concern for explicit meaning, for internal consistency, and for protecting the boundaries of self and outlook. It heightens one's own self-consciousness. In terms of our understanding symbols, it puts a premium on the interpretative activity of the knower. It minimizes any emphasis on the symbol's or myth's power to transform our understanding. Thus, the knowing, inquiring subject brings to light and controls the object—the uninterpreted symbol, ritual, or myth, which only rarely can act on us.

As we turn now to some quotes from an interview subject representative of an early Stage 4, it is important to keep in mind the distinction between the *content* and the *structure* or *form* of faith knowing. The respondent I am about to introduce is no longer religious in any traditional sense—at least in his own view. Many of the features that mark his answers as representative of Stage 4 are heightened by the fact that he is a graduate student, and a graduate student in psychology at that. He is twenty-two years of age and recently married. Plainly he is what Jung would call a "thinking type." By his own admission, his beliefs and ideas are in flux and his lifestyle, in terms of marriage and profession, is in its early stages of consolidation. Yet the standpoint and way of moving into these areas and tasks seems clear. It is that clarity—that pattern of thinking, evaluating, and committing—which constitutes the Stage 4 character of his faith outlook. Conducted three years ago, when we still began our interviews with a fairly directive question, our respondent, Mr. E, was asked: "How would you describe your religion, your lifestyle, or your system of values?"

He: Well, as for my religion, if you take it from the point of view of organized religion, there basically is none. I was born a Catholic but don't practice any formal religion, ritual, or anything like that. . . . I live my life the way I think I should—that doesn't depend at all on the religious formulations of any group or religious organization, and my values are just what seems right to me. I rejected the values of many organized religions and hold some values which are contrary to not only organized religion but to society as a whole.

I: Then your values would seem very much a part of your lifestyle?

He: Yes, I mean, they are my lifestyle. It's not like I act—or before I act I think "What do my values have to say about this?" The values are more or less assumed or more or less there, and I act in accordance with them. There is no dichotomy or split between what I think is right and what I do. I do what I think is right so my lifestyle is my values.

I: . . . How would you judge that this value system or lifestyle makes you different from other people?

He: Well, first of all there is a question of how do I differ from other people? That depends who the people are. Some people obviously have moral codes based on organized, you know, simulated schema such as the Ten Commandments or what the United States culture considers to be right or wrong, or lawful or unlawful. Other people don't care about law or commandments at all, so I am different than they are because I adhere to a schema but it is not organized or part of a formal organization. . . .

In these passages, we see several features that are characteristic of Stage 4. First, there is a high degree of reflective self-consciousness. Whereas Mrs. M in our previous interview seemed to be articulating a considerable amount of her self-reflection for the first time, Mr. E has clearly and consistently devoted time and energy to self-monitoring reflection. Second, Mr. E reflects on his way of seeing and valuing as an explicit system, one that has determinate boundaries, is distinguishable from those of others, and whose content is capable of internal differentiation and testing for congruence and consistency. Third, as is often true of those with newly equilibrated Stage 4 outlooks, Mr. E tends to dichotomize his present position from all that went before, thereby excluding the influences of family and of his religious upbringing and education. Finally, although there are hardly enough data to make the case firmly, Mr. E, in taking the perspectives of persons and groups with different lifestyles or value systems than his own, seems to illustrate Stage 4's tendency to caricature such competing strategies, both due to insufficient experience and knowledge and to the somewhat defensive character of his own as yet incompletely tested and established structures.

The next passage from Mr. E's interview shows us how the person at Stage 4 differentiates between self and outlook, between identity and value system. It also illustrates how people at Stage 4 in general contrast with those at Stage 3, employ abstract concepts in describing themselves, their personal changes, and what they are experiencing. Mr. E was asked: "Where do you feel your values or beliefs are changing? Are you aware of a restlessness or of continuing change?"

He: Well, as much as I have given the impression or might have given the impression that the value system is relatively stable, it is in a constant state of flux and there are a lot of concepts such as reincarnation, karma, the whole concept of the afterlife, people's purposes on earth and things like that which I am in the process of integrating into that scheme. That integration is not fully successful yet. I mean, it is not completed. . . . Right now I am in a stage where I am leaving behind a purely pragmatic atheism. I am in the middle of a sort of a humanistic, people-oriented value system and I am heading towards a more transcendental, spiritualistic value system which incorporates, I think, those human values.

It is tempting to relegate words like these to the catchall category "head-trip." Clearly, Mr. E is leading with his head, and his head is imaginatively speculating far beyond where he has yet tested his convictions and values in the everyday struggle of wins and losses, or against shocks and unexpected events. Though present here in a somewhat inflated form, there is in Stage 4 an excessive reliance upon and trust in conscious processes and controls. This feature is part of the strength of this stage, and is a necessary correlate of the new quality of self-responsibility and autonomy which Stage 4 assumes.

When asked about his current attitudes towards the teachings of Jesus, Mr. E's response illustrated Stage 4's application of a "reductive hermeneutic" in the sphere of religious symbolism. It is also another instance of Stage 4's assimilation of "objective" content to subjective structures:

He: The teachings of Jesus are fine. I can buy them. At times they require some strain. I think that the picture that the church has drawn of Jesus is sometimes a little too wishy-washy or namby-pamby. He seemed effeminate when in actuality he was probably a very strong, virile person. The church portrays him as passive or impassive, apathetical almost, and in fact he seems to have been almost rebellious and an energetic person. So that I think the teachings of Christ fit very well with my general philosophy or set of moral values. I think that the way that the church has portrayed Christ requires a little modification. In other words, I can't take Christ as the church has made him out. I have to reinterpret him —make him more human—before I can accept him. But I can very easily.

In the last passage I want to quote from Mr. E there is a

mitigating recognition of some of the gaps between the espoused and actual values in his life, and of the mysteries of life that spill beyond his conceptual frameworks. In this passage he is trying to account for the motivating forces at work in his own life:

He: . . . I may not be—I may not do what I want as much as I may appear to. I view myself as much more confined and socialized than perhaps I give the impression of being. I have certain goals. There are certain things I want to do in life and these require me to go through certain rituals like getting a college diploma or getting a Ph.D. or something like that. So I am not doing what I want totally. I am giving in to society so I will get what I want eventually or do what I want eventually. . . . As for the motivating force—there probably is one. What it is I can't put my finger on. Now like I said, I am coming to believe in reincarnation and also that life has purpose not so much after the fact as before the fact. . . . The soul in its progression towards actualization and development goes through a series of reincarnations, each of which teaches it lessons about itself or about life, how it can improve itself and become more like the ideal, which we might call God. . . . So the motivating force may be interpreted as the knowledge of the soul. It is in a situation to grow in a certain way, to develop certain habits or traits or whatever, and that is just what it has to do.

The *contents* of Mr. E's faith outlook will likely continue to undergo amendment as he works on at his profession, his marriage, and at the shaping of his life. The *structures* of thinking, feeling, and valuing which constitute his way of positioning himself in life may remain for the rest of his life pretty much as we have glimpsed them in these brief state-ments. On the other hand, after ten or fifteen or twenty years of "making meaning" with this structural set, Mr. E may find himself evolving towards a new and more flexible system of structuring faith patterns. When and if that evolution occurs, it is our bet that structurally it will involve the emergence of something akin to Stage 5, to which we now turn.

Stage 5:
Paradoxical-Consolidative

What Stage 4 struggled to make explicit and firm—as to the boundaries and inner structures of one's makeup and outlook —Stage 5 must make porous and multiplex. Stage 5 involves the integration of many dimensions that were suppressed or evaded in Stage 4's self-certainty. Stage 5 involves a fresh reclaiming and reworking of one's past. It involves an open-ness to the sometimes anarchic voices of one's "deep self," or what Jung calls the "objective psyche." Equally important, Stage 5 requires a critical coming to terms with one's *social* unconscious: the myths, norms, ideal images, and prejudices built deeply into the self-system by virtue of one's upbringing within a particular social class, religious tradition, regional outlook, ethnic identity, national community, or the like.[19]

As we have seen in previous stages, a person's ability to take the perspectives of other individuals and groups is directly and reciprocally related to his or her capacity for self-reflection. Because Stage 5 involves a multidimensional self-knowledge, it also involves a qualitative leap in both the comprehensiveness and accuracy of a person's mutual perspective-taking with other persons and groups.

When this process becomes a natural part of an individual, "truth" comes to be a much more paradoxical reality than it was in Stage 4. Truth must be apprehended from a variety of standpoints. Stage 5 embraces and maintains the apparent contradictions or tensions that arise when truth is viewed from diverse perspectives. Though this often requires living with paradox, Stage 5 faith sees it as required by the character of truth.

Two common misunderstandings of Stage 5 must be guarded against. First, we must remind ourselves that faith-knowing at Stage 5, though more complex than at previous stages, both carries forward the capacities of previous stages and continues to involve a blend of thought *and* feeling, of reason *and* passion, of cognition *and* commitment. Second, we must not assume that the structural operations of faith at Stage 5 are available only as the result either of genius or of formal training in philosophy or theology.[20] The structural characteristics of Stage 5 are not a *content* that can be taught, but rather are the products of one's reflective interaction with other people and with the conditions of one's life. It draws its meaning from the images or visions provided by those traditions of life wisdom that are available or found usable.

Transition to Stage 5 is rare before age thirty. There is some evidence that persons who are disadvantaged and who suffer class, racial, sexual or ethnic discrimination and oppression—and who have previously made the difficult transition from Stage 3 to Stage 4—frequently confront Stage 5 issues and construct Stage 5 perspectives earlier than do more advantaged persons. This is not surprising, since survival and coping, for such persons, depend upon being able to take the perspective of the dominant and advantaged groups and their representatives. Also, it seems that compassion and empathy for the victims of suffering and injustice come more readily to those who have experienced them than to those who overtly or unconsciously benefit from them. In any case, Stage 5 requires that one know suffering and loss, responsibility and failure, and the grief that is an inevitable part of having made irrevocable commitments of life and energy. Age thirty is a minimal age. Stage 5 most often is a midlife development if it comes at all.

Now to the chart and its categories on Stage 5.

A. In Stage 5, formal operations, as applied to the construction and maintenance of self and outlook, exhibit a *dialectical* style. Attuned to paradox and tension, thinking in Stage 5 embraces polarities, tending to see both (or the many) sides of an issue or situation simultaneously. Also, Stage 5 faith-knowing involves a more critical self-awareness and an intentional incorporation of the modes of one's own subjectivity into thinking and judgment.

B. Drawing on multiple perspectives, an individual in Stage 5 constructs and maintains a pluralistic model of *coherence* in reality. He or she resists forced syntheses or reductionist interpretations and is prepared to live with ambiguity, mystery, wonder, and apparent irrationalities.

C. Role-taking at Stage 5 brings augmented comprehensiveness and accuracy in taking the perspectives of other people and groups. This involves suspending or transcending one's own views in an effort to feel and grasp the full impact of others' experiences. There is thus a vulnerability in Stage 5 role-taking, a readiness to risk the kind of openness that could lead to the altering of one's own perspectives, values, and/or material conditions, to seeing one's own position or that of one's group from the standpoint of others.

D. *Authority* for the person at Stage 5 must meet the critical tests implied by multiple perspectives, comprehensive role-taking, increased self-awareness, and disciplined subjectivity. Of course, the criteria for authority operating at earlier stages are still present and active. They are qualified at Stage 5, however, by the further internalization of authority made possible by the structures of awareness we have been describing.

E. In Stage 5, one seeks expanded identification with and inclusion of groups and classes other than one's own in the determination of moral responsibility. Stage 5 is ready for a community identification beyond tribal, racial, class, or ideological boundaries. To be genuine, it must consistently press toward such community inclusiveness in its conduct of individual and group life. This means that a person at Stage 5, when his or her attitude is genuine, will feel a special commitment to struggling for and securing justice for all people and groups.

F. The form of *moral judgment* at Stage 5 is principled, and its reasoning and acting on principle are less distorted by class and group biases than are those of Stage 4. At Stage 5 there is a consistent higher-law perspective which may exhibit the forms of either Kohlberg's Stage 5 or 6. In the understanding and pursuit of justice at Stage 5, the indicative (seeing what justice requires) and the imperative (doing what justice requires) are inseparable.

G. In relation to symbol, myth, and ritual, Stage 5 includes but moves beyond the limiting interpretations of Stage 4. It establishes or reclaims a relationship to myth, symbol, and ritual in which the affective and esthetic import are rejoined with the ideational content and are allowed to make an impact on their own terms. Ricoeur calls this a *recollective* interpretative style, and characterizes the combination of disciplined subjectivity with the postcritical participation in the symbolic it involves as a *second naivete*. I like to say that at Stage 5 one "sees through" the symbolic medium in a double sense: critically, one sees through its partiality, relativity, and ambiguity. But postcritically—and simultaneously—one sees through the symbolic by intentionally submitting to an *envisioning*—a new way of seeing—by the symbol, thereby grasping life and reality in fresh depth and enlarged possibility.

Stage 5 is relatively rare. The interview I have chosen to represent this stage is that of a thirty-six-year-old woman, Mrs. B. She is an educator, an artist, and a political activist. She is married, without children. In the interview, as she is recounting some of the central influences on the formation of her values, she is asked: "Did you feel, and do you feel, that your values *should* hold true or do hold true for all other people as well?"

She: No. And that's difficult, because I believe *some* of my values should hold true for other people. But I don't believe that I can *impose* my values on other people. (Why?) Because *they* have as much right as I do to choose and decide their own course and what they value. I have no more right to impose on them than they do to impose on me. On the other hand, I have a responsibility—and this is a priority that increases as I grow older and know more, and learn more—I have an obligation to, to express my values and in a sense teach what I have learned from experience, as well as learned from other people. . . . There are some times when one can *express* one's feelings and put oneself in a precarious or uncomfortable position. . . . But I have to place a high value on expressing what I feel. And when I see something that is *damaging*, hurtful, restrictive *to* human beings . . . I feel it is an obligation and a high value of mine to talk about it, to express it, to say what I feel. . . . What I'm trying to say is that the internal values that I hold are only, I can only experience them and test them in talking about them, in relating them and living them. And sometimes that involves risk to— it has even involved risk to my personal safety. . . .

I: Is there a community of people who share your outlook?

She: I think there's a community of people that share it, but I don't *know* all of them. I'm connected to them, in a sense, through a *spiritual* sense. I can, I *sense* it in some people. . . . The community is not defined in space; it's defined in time and consciousness.

In the interview, Mrs. B relates a number of incidents in which her value commitments have been tested, including the dissolution of her first marriage. Her thirty-six years have brought her more than the usual number of experiences of death, of community conflict, and of demands for leadership. Reflecting on the death by suicide of her mother, she said:

She: Perhaps the most important thing that I have learned from that is to, to realize how temporal life is. What you value most must be acted upon. And if you put it off in the context of impossible, otherworldly, unattainable, then you can just, in a sense, *die*—destroy the world by not accepting it, not acknowledging it, not being part of it. So in a sense the alternative to committing suicide is to kill the world around you. So that you screen out the world; you sift out, until you only work on what is immediate to you. I think many people do this out of fear.

Some of the paradoxical quality of Stage 5 finds expression in the next quote from Mrs. B's interview. In this response, we also see evidence of a perspective-taking which identifies with diverse types of people and groups and, in addition, includes other nonhuman aspects of being. Mrs. B was asked what a proper or adequate view of life requires. She replied:

She: Well, keeping a perspective, but also being conscious of keeping a perspective. Being conscious that there is that constant dichotomy of the absurd and the real, and understanding that. At the same time, living within the context of my very physical world. . . . Being conscious of hundreds of thousands of other living things. Millions of other people, and the possibility of billions of other worlds and planets. . . . You know, keeping an understanding of myself in relation to the Universe. And the finite in relation to the infinite. And *me* being finite and all that other being infinite. How to find a way of continuing in time, being able to do what I value most without hurting what I also value. . . . It's very difficult.

In trying to articulate her hopes for herself and for others, Mrs. B draws on her artist's creativity, employing the symbolism of a tree:

She: To me a tree is a very strong picture or symbol. . . . As it grows taller and wider, its roots grow deeper and deeper so it's expanding in both directions. And the bark, at the same time, gets thicker and thicker. (What is the bark for you?) The bark for me . . . isn't the important part of the tree, but I'll answer your question. The bark for me is the, is the protection against the kinds of things that are accidental, that I have no control over. The leaves are reaching out for nourishment, are blossoming, seeking the sun. The roots are constantly reaching down for nourishment and for water and life-supporting kinds of things. But the bark is important. The bark is the every-day living. When someone walks up to a tree and rips the bark off the tree, no matter how deep the roots are, or how tall the crown of the tree may be, it can die. It can be ended; it can be severed. Maybe the roots are, for me, my past and a whole collective awareness or con-sciousness of a past—a past not only of myself, but of my ancestors, past life, past traditions, knowledge. Maybe the leaves to me are my aspirations, my hopes, my wishes. The *best* I can be, the closest I can come to the sun, to the Universe, to the stars, to the wind. All these natural symbols to me are very important. But the bark of the tree is my living, finite body. And . . . the stuff that goes on every day. And in that sense the tree can't really affect that much. It's stable. It's very con-fined. But through the trunk, through the tree, through the bark, grows the stuff that *can* come out. And the seeds that can fall. And birds can live there. It can be-come an umbrella for people who don't want to get wet, underneath.

At the end of the interview Mrs. B struggles to express what to her is most important in life. In her answer, the polar alternation between the active and the contemplative moments in life are held together. As earlier with the polari-ties of the absurd and the real, the finite and the infinite, for her the tension between the active and the contemplative must be maintained and not collapsed in either direction:

She: I sometimes think that moving to a rock on the top of a mountain in Nepal might be the answer. To sit and meditate and . . . communicate with a totally spiritual world. But to me that isn't possible, because to me what is important is what is alive and what is around me. I want to maintain a balance between that meditative, spiritual part and the real, the real—the suffering, the anger, the very heavy part of the world. To me, in order to *live*, . . . I have to stay here. I can't go off and meditate and go into the spiritual. . . . The goal is to bring the two together continually over and over and over again in a spiral that goes up and up and up and incorporates past, present, and future. . . . It's like being a river going by a pyramid. A river: the pyramid is past, present, and future. And it's constantly going, you know, through and around and under; and the sky and the spirit and the earth, and the nurturing, and all that.

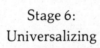

Stage 6:
Universalizing

In order to characterize Stage 6, we must focus more sharply on the dialectical or paradoxical features of Stage 5 faith-knowing and faith-being. At Stage 5, one can see injustice in sharply etched terms because of an enlarged awareness of the demands of justice and the implications of those demands. One can recognize partial truths and their limitations because of a more comprehensive vision of truth. One can appreciate and cherish symbols, myths, and rituals in new depth because of an increased apprehension of the depth of the reality to which the symbols refer and which they mediate. At this stage, one experiences the fractures and divisions of the human family with vivid pain because of an apprehension of a possible inclusive commonwealth of being. The views of Stage 5 remain paradoxical or divided, however, because one is caught between these universalizing apprehensions and the need to preserve one's own well-being. In this situation of paradox, the person at Stage 5 must act and not be paralyzed. But at that stage one acts out of conflicting loyalties. A readiness to spend and be spent on behalf of others is limited by concern for one's own, or one's family, or one's group survival. Perceptions of justice outreach the readiness to sacrifice self for the sake of justice and in the spirit of love.‡‡

The transition to Stage 6 involves an overcoming of this paradox through a moral and ascetic *actualization* of the universalizing apprehensions. Heedless of the personal threats that it involves, the individual at Stage 6 becomes a disciplined, activist *incarnation* of the imperatives of absolute love and justice which at Stage 5 are only partially grasped. This person engages in spending and being spent in order to transform present reality in the direction of a transcendent actuality.

Persons best described by Stage 6 exhibit qualities which shake our usual criteria of normalcy. Their lack of attention to self-preservation and the vividness of their taste and feel for transcendent moral and religious actuality give their actions and words an extraordinary and often unpredictable quality. In their devotion to universalizing compassion they may offend our parochial perceptions of justice. In penetrating through the usual human obsession with survival, security, and significance, they threaten measured standards of righteousness, goodness, and prudence. Their enlarged visions of universal community disclose the narrowness of

‡‡ *The connection between love and justice is further explored and clarified by Fowler in the Dialogue section.—Ed.*

our tribal identities. Their leadership initiatives, which often involve strategies of nonviolent suffering and of ultimate respect for life, constitute affronts to our pragmatism, our realism, and our usual notions of relevance. It is little wonder, then, that persons best described by Stage 6 frequently become martyrs to the visions they incarnate. §§

Let's examine the shape of our categories at Stage 6.

A. The readiness to relinquish oneself for the sake of love and justice at the moral and religious levels also involves a significant epistemological shift. A feeling of *oneness* or *unity* with the intent or "character" of the ultimate environment radically changes the status and importance of the self. At Stage 6, formal operational thought is brought to bear on self, on others, and on outlook. But because the self has now found its ground *in* and identity *with* Being, its style of composing a sense of ultimate environment is synthetic and unitive. There is a union of opposites that is no longer experienced as paradoxical. This is because the knowing self is operationally identified or at one with transcendent actuality.

B. An ultimate coherence informs one's outlook at Stage 6. This coherence—a complex, and plural unity—centers on a oneness beyond but inclusive of the manyness of Being.

C. Role-taking at Stage 6 involves taking the perspective of an ideal, inclusive commonwealth of Being. With that perspective, a person at Stage 6 informs acts so as to respect the true potentials or ends of the constituents of Being.

D. Authority inheres, for Stage 6, in a heart and mind purified of egoistic striving and attentive to the requirements of Being.

§§*It will come as no surprise that Martin Luther King, Jr., and Mahatma Gandhi are included in this number. I would also want to include such figures as Mother Teresa of Calcutta, Abraham Lincoln, and Dag Hammarskjold.*

E. *The bounds of social awareness* become universal, but not merely in an abstract sense. There is a profound regard for all Being. This regard is capable of becoming and remaining concrete and effective at any moment or in any relation.

F. Loyalty to Being is the fundamental principle of moral reasoning. Strategies of action both serve this loyalty and remain consistent with it as a principle.

G. Symbols are transparent to the depth of the actuality they mediate for Stage 6. Stage 6 persons are profound shapers and regenerators of symbols, due to the immediate quality of their relation to and participation in transcendent actuality.

I am always conscious, as I try to write about Stage 6, that my words are at best a kind of abstract poetry. Stage 6 can really be grasped only through the lives of those who incarnate it. And then it spills over the edges of all our categories. I am not sure that Stage 6 really describes or requires any basic structural advance beyond Stage 5. But its radical relativization of the self as center and its self-spending action on behalf of a universal commonwealth of Being result in so dramatic a redirection of the structures of faith that it constitutes a qualitative revolution.

To conclude this overview of the stages of faith, and as a kind of completion of the journey, I want to share some excerpts from an interview in which the spirit and structure of Stage 6 become visible. Having already described the characteristics of the stage, my comments on the interview will be spare. Our companion is elderly, a celibate member of a religious order. He is not a widely known public figure like the other examples of Stage 6 I have mentioned. For the circle of persons who know him and who have been influenced by him, however, his life has been a source of liberating insight and example, and a generative fountain of courageous joy.

Voluntarily suggested by his younger colleagues as a person who to them seemed most representative of the spirit of Stage 6, he was interviewed by one of my students:

I: At the present, what would you say gives your life meaning?

He: God, the giver.

I: Do you want to explain that a little bit?

He: Well, I think that is basic to Christianity, and understood well enough, God is the only person in this universe who is truly liberal: in the sense that he cannot receive anything, and he does not *want* to receive anything. God is the sheer giver and complete unselfishness. He is the God of love because he is the God of holiness. And he cannot give unless we are willing to receive. And the problems of the human race come from setting up idols and trying to conform everything to our selfish and avaricious ideas and ideals, and then exploiting other people and blocking them off if they are not of our own background or outlook; and I think that is basic to my whole life.

I: What do you see as the purpose or purposes of human life?

He: It's receiving from God what he wants to give. That is the purpose of human life. And we are constituted by an aspiration for union with God to the highest degree that we can receive him. That is what human life is all about. And we have that deep aspiration covered up with all of these ephemeral drives and looking here, there, and the other place for something that will fulfill us, and masking the deepest aspiration which is for God and for love of our neighbor, which is by a sacrificial love. "Sacrificial" does not mean giving up things: it means a unifying love which we receive only from God and his inner dynamism, because we are all selfish and sinful and therefore to love members of the human race who are not in themselves lovable. And growth is in the realization that we do this not through our own power, but through the transformation of our spirit by the spirit of God.

I: Then you see people as the instrument or the vessel for this love; is that what I'm hearing?

He: Yes. And everybody is either in some process of opening up to love or cutting it off, and that is the real problem of our human situation.

I: Why do some people cut off this love?

He: Because, well, radically I think it is because of their experience. Their home life, either terrible selfishness or lack of outgoing love, and then in their environmental situation where you have people who never experience as a class anything but inhumanity and cruelty from their fellow people. Then perhaps worse is the drive for power in people who are extremely talented, but they are using that only for their own self-aggrandizement, and manipulating and dominating other people. . . .

I: Okay, so, you'd say—If I say, what are the beliefs or attitudes or values that dominate your life, it would be the value of love, and the purpose of being. . . .

He: Well, the value of love that does not spring from my inner resources alone, but only through the inner transformation of the spirit. It isn't from God or Christ looked upon as a model; it is the realization of solidarity with him that he's available to give me a new life. And —but the inner wellspring of that is the constant, growing realization that I am being gifted more and more. Therefore there's a receiving radically; but it is a dynamic receiving. It isn't an automatic or a quietistic sort of thing. It is an impulsion to love without constantly looking for feedback or return. And that is available to anyone.

I: Are there some beliefs or values that all people ought to have and act on?

He: Yes, radically, I think. And I think the radical belief and value that none of us is an isolated island and that on a sheer worldly viewpoint that no one can make it on his or her own. And then a growth of the realization that "making it" does not mean the accumulation of wealth and consumerism and all that sort of thing. It is the growth in love, and particularly for those who are less fortunate. Those, I think, are the basic values that should guide a human life. But they need to be filled in with all that I said before.

I: Are there some systems of religious beliefs that are truer than others . . .?

He: I don't—I think we are dealing here radically with mystery, and mystery is incapable of systematization. But I think the deepest, radical aspiration of every human being *is* a gift of God, and it is an impulse toward union with God and with our fellow human beings. Now in each one's situation, the use of all human resources, of intelligence and affectivity and sensitivity—that is a judgment . . . that each one has to make for him or her self. And I think that it is foolish to try to systematize that and to force everyone into a groove. But I think that the mystery of God's call is *in* everyone, either more or less explicit. And if people followed that radical inclination, then their own individual tendencies and drives would lead toward greater union and harmony, but without systematization. I think that the difficulty with systematization is the dogmatism of setting up one philosophy and one way of life, and then trying to impose that on others as if it were an absolute, as if that were taking the place of mystery. And nothing can take the place of mystery. But by mystery I don't mean projection of your own mind; I mean a realization tested in practice that I am being consumed by an unselfish love and a realization that that is not my own, and it's beyond my power. I guess—and yet, it is my own because it is not making me an automaton. It is the only freedom that a human being is really capable of. It is the freedom of subjection in a personal way to a God who is everything and apart from whom I and everybody else are nothing, and on a dead-end street that is going to lead to frustration and despair and hopelessness. . . .

I: So what do you—in terms of what happens after death —what do you think that is? What is death?

He: I think that death is the transition from this visible universe as we see it to the realm of God, and into complete human fulfillment in the most intimate union that an infinite God can give with himself and that is surely a gratuitous gift. But the gift of grace in this life and glory are not two distinct things. We're not working for that as something to be added afterwards. I believe very firmly in the Johannine idea of the realized eschatology: he who believes in me *has* eternal life, and that the indwelling of the spirit is a personal transformation like the seed. If you had two zygotes, one of an anthropoid ape and one of a human being, probably the most experienced zoologist could not tell the difference without all kinds of microscopes, and even then I don't know. But the difference between the two is enormous. The zygote of the ape can *never* have the slightest spark of spiritual love, outgoing love for another; whereas the zygote of the human is incapable of being human unless it attains to that type of love, spiritual ideal as well as intellectual, and affecting his whole sensitivity and union with other spiritual beings. But this goal of God to involve us in his inner trinitarian life is a gift that surpasses the gift of creation of us even as the apex of visible creation made to the image and likeness of God. Because even that is the action of God as an artist. It's a production, but the artist, much as he may love his work, does not think that his life is given to that work. It is an attempt to express his sense of beauty, but I don't think that any artist is ever satisfied. But the action of God in Christian life is not that type of action. It far transcends that. It is God entering into our lowliness, and it is a communicative and a unitive love. It is drawing us into his family and is best expressed by John 6:44 in the heart of mystery here: no one can come to me unless the father draw him, *ean me helkusēi*. That word *helkusēi* means an ineffable attraction that we feel within ourselves towards the transcendental, but the transcendental not as an abstraction, but as the deepest personal love imaginable. And that is what faith is. . . .

Table 1.3
FAITH: THE STRUCTURAL-DEVELOPMENTAL APPROACH

STAGES	A. FORM OF LOGIC (MODIFIED PIAGET)
1. Intuitive-Projective	Preoperational
2. Mythic-Literal	Concrete operational
3. Synthetic-Conventional	Early formal operations
4. Individuative-Reflexive	Formal operations (Dichotomizing)
5. Paradoxical-Consolidative	Formal operations (Dialectical)
6. Universalizing	Formal operations (Synthetic)

STAGES	D. LOCUS OF AUTHORITY
1. Intuitive-Projective	Located in and derivative of child's attachment/dependent relationships to parents or parent-like adults. Criteria of size, power, and visible signs of authority.
2. Mythic-Literal	Located in incumbents of authority roles and made (more or less) salient by personal proximity and trust-inspiring qualities
3. Synthetic-Conventional	Located in traditional or con-sensual perspective of valued group and in persons authorized or recognized as personally worthy representatives.

B. FORM OF WORLD COHERENCE	C. ROLE-TAKING (MODIFIED SELMAN)
Episodic	Rudimentary empathy
Narrative-dramatic	Simple perspective-taking
Tacit system, symbolic mediation	Mutual role-taking (interpersonal), "third person" perspective
Explicit system, conceptual mediation	Mutual, with self-selected group or class
Multisystemic, symbolic *and* conceptual mediation	Mutual, with groups, classes, and traditions other than one's own
Unitive actuality, "One beyond the many"	Mutual, with the commonwealth of Being

4. Individuative-Reflexive	Located in personally appropriated pragmatic or ideologically established perspectives and in spokespersons or group procedures or outlooks consistent with such perspectives.
5. Paradoxical-Consolidative	Located in the dialectic between critically self-chosen beliefs, norms, and values and those maintained in the reflective claims of other persons and groups and in various expressions of cumulative human wisdom.
6. Universalizing	Building on all that went before, authority now located in the judgment purified of egoistic striving and attentive to the requirements of Being.

STAGES	E. BOUNDS OF SOCIAL AWARENESS
1. Intuitive-Projective	Family, primal others
2. Mythic-Literal	"Those like us" (in familial, ethnic, racial, class and religious terms)
3. Synthetic-Conventional	Conformity to class norms and interests
4. Individuative-Reflexive	Self-aware adherence to chosen class norms and interests
5. Paradoxical-Consolidative	Critical awareness of and transcendence of class norms and interests
6. Universalizing	Trans-class awareness and identification

F. FORM OF MORAL JUDGMENT (MODIFIED KOHLBERG)	G. ROLE OF SYMBOLS
Punishment-reward	Magical-Numinous
Instrumental Hedonism	One-dimensional, literal
Interpersonal concord Law and Order ↕	Multidimensional, conventional
Reflective relativism or class-biased universalism	Critical translation into ideas
Principled Higher Law (Universal-critical)	Postcritical rejoining of symbolic nuance and ideational content
Loyalty to Being	Transparency of symbols .

References: First Presentation

1. Erik Erikson, *Childhood and Society* (New York: W. W. Norton, 1950, 1963), Ch. 7. See also *Identity and the Life Cycle, Identity, Youth and Crisis,* and *Young Man Luther,* all by Erikson.

2. See my "Faith Liberation and Human Development," Lecture I, in *The Foundation* (Atlanta: Gammon Theological Seminary), Vol. 79 (1974), for a fuller discussion of the relations of faith, religion and belief.

3. The influences of both Martin Buber and George Herbert Mead, among others, are gratefully acknowledged here.

4. See Josiah Royce, *The Sources of Religious Insight* (New York: 1912), Ch. V. See H. Richard Niebuhr, *Radical Monotheism and Western Culture* (New York: Harper & Row, 1960) and *The Responsible Self* (New York: Harper & Row, 1963). On Niebuhr see also the present author's *To See the Kingdom* (Nashville: Abingdon, 1974), Ch. V.

5. See Gordon D. Kaufman, *An Essay on Theological Method* (Scholars Press, 1975), especially Ch. II, "Theology as Construction."

6. For a sparkling statement of this insight, see William F. Lynch, S.J., *Images of Faith* (Notre Dame Press, 1973).

7. Richard R. Niebuhr's *Experiential Religion* (New York: 1972), offers a subtle, brilliant development of a perspective much like that I am offering here. I acknowledge my indebtedness and urge others to tackle Niebuhr's book.

8. For the best overall introduction to Piaget's extensive writings, see Herbert Ginsberg and Sylvia Opper, *Piaget's Theory of Intellectual Development* (New York: 1969). Piaget's *Six Psychological Studies* (New York: 1967) provides readable pieces by Piaget himself.

9. For an overview of the critical discussions of cross-cultural efforts to validate the claims of universality for Piaget's structural stages, see Patricia Teague Ashton, "Cross Cultural Piagetian Research: An Experimental Perspective," in *Harvard Educational Review,* Vol. 45, No. 4 (November 1975), pp. 475-506. See also Patricia M. Greenfield and Jerome Bruner, "Culture and Cognitive Growth," in David A. Goslin, ed., *Handbook of Socialization Theory and Research* (Chicago: 1969), pp. 633-657.

10. For valuable statements of Kohlberg's theory, see Kohlberg, "Stage and Sequence: The Cognitive-Developmental Approach to Socialization," in David A. Goslin, ed., *Handbook of Socialization Theory*

and Research, pp. 347-48; Kohlberg, "Continuities and Discontinuities in Childhood and Adult Moral Development Revisited," in Baltes and Schaie, eds., *Life-Span Developmental Psychology: Research and Theory* (New York: Holt, 1972); Kohlberg and R. Mayer, "Development as the Aim of Education," in *Harvard Educational Review*, Vol. 42, No. 4 (November 1972); and Kohlberg, "Moral Stages and Moralization," in Thomas Lickona, ed., *Moral Development and Behavior* (New York: Holt, 1976).

11. See especially Kohlberg, "From Is to Ought: How to Commit the Naturalistic Fallacy and Get Away with it in the Study of Moral Development," in Mischel, ed., *Cognitive Development and Epistemology* (New York: Academic Press, 1971).

12. See Paul Tillich, *Dynamics of Faith* (New York: Harper & Row, 1957); H. Richard Niebuhr, *Radical Monotheism and Western Culture* (New York: Harper & Row, 1960); and Wilfred Cantwell Smith, *The Meaning and End of Religion* (New York: Harper & Row).

13. See Edward L. Whitmont, *The Symbolic Quest* (New York: Harper Colophon Books, 1973), for a comprehensive introduction to Jung's ideas and terminology.

14. See Robert N. Bellah, *Beyond Belief* (New York: Harper & Row, 1970), Ch. 2.

15. See Fowler, "Stages in Faith: The Structural Developmental Perspective," in Thomas Hennessey, ed., *Studies in Moral Development* (Paramus, N.J.: Paulist Press, 1976); and Fowler, "Faith Development Theory and the Aims of Religious Socialization," in Gloria Durka and Joan-Marie Smith, eds., *Emerging Issues in Religious Education* (Paulist Press, 1976).

16. Robert L. Selman, "The Developmental Conceptions of Interpersonal Relations," Publication of the Harvard-Judge Baker Social Reasoning Project, December 1974, Vols. I and II. See also Selman, "Social-Cognitive Understanding," in Thomas Lickona, ed., *Moral Development and Behavior* (New York: Holt, 1976).

17. Maurice Sendak, *Where the Wild Things Are* (New York: Harper & Row, 1963).

18. See Paul Ricoeur, *The Symbolism of Evil* (Boston: Beacon, 1969), especially pp. 347 ff.

19. For a challenging expansion of this idea, see Russell Jacoby, *Social Amnesia* (Boston: Beacon Press, 1975).

20. A powerful illustration of this point is provided by the illiterate Southern black sharecropper Nate Shaw whose life-stories are transcribed (from taped interviews) by Theodore Rosengarten in *All God's Dangers* (New York: Alfred Knopf, 1974). Shaw clearly and powerfully embodies Stage 5.

Second Presentation:
Sam Keen*
Body/Faith:
Trust, Dissolution & Grace

I want to talk about the nature of trust and the stages along life's way. We could as easily entitle this chapter "Trust and Carnality," or "Animal Faith and Incarnation," or "The Stages of Trust," or even, and maybe best of all, "The Holy Spirit is a Wild Dove, Not a Tame Pigeon."

By way of orientation, I offer two aphorisms that can be held onto like threads in a labyrinth, or kept sight of like two polar stars to guide us on the quest for trust:

1. Trust begins when we stop putting everything into pigeon holes and start following the wild dove.

2. A trusting life is like a living sun, not like a dead planet; it is made up of a series of explosions.

In my critique of and discussion with Jim Fowler, I am going to proceed on the assumption that, as Karl Jaspers said, "loving combat" is the highest form of communication. I trust we are friends and coworkers; therefore, I am challenging his ideas fiercely. In the game of ideas, we should play hard, neither asking nor giving quarter.

*All notes are the author's unless otherwise indicated.

A Difference of Approach:

Dionysius and Apollo

The first thing I would like to talk about is our difference of approach. According to the wisdom of the Greeks, Dionysius and Apollo shared a temple during various months of the year. This was their way of acknowledging that there were different styles of life and different modes of doing things. Apollo was the god of reason, rationality, light, moderation, and intellect. Dionysius was the god of wine and excess, passion and immoderation. Generally speaking, Jim's approach is Apollonian and mine is Dionysian.

Jim Fowler's idealization of faith as a form of world coherence is a professorial typology of human development in which everybody ends up like a professor with a coherent view of the world. This notion of faith is largely masculine and is biased toward an intellectual way of being in the world. It makes little room for other types of persons, for what Jung referred to as sensation, intuitive, or feeling types.

We are all prone to ideological statements. Therefore, we should apply the Heisenberg principle to our own intellectual work. The Heisenberg principle for personality theorists could be stated this way: whoever looks at a phenomenon distorts it because what he sees is always filtered through the prejudices of his own peculiar modes of perception.

I admit that my own perspective is also ideological. It is merely a different ideology. I am not pure. But my taste is for a different kind of excess. James Fowler and I are different types of sinners.

Here are some of the different forms of sin I prefer. Jim's approach to the problem of faith and trust is predominantly cognitive, intellectual, institutional, and symbolic. I emphasize the conative (wish-desire-fantasy), the affective (feeling), and the carnal (sensual) elements of faith and trust. I do not even use the word *faith* unless I slip. I prefer *trust*, which is a gut word, not a head word.

Jim is Apollonian in stressing the similarity of faith to the ordering principle. I am Dionysian in my emphasis on the relationship of trust to the passional and the disordering principles in the personality. Jim points to the continuity of faith and culture; I stress its discontinuity. His dominant working image is that faith is the glue that keeps the ego together. To quote him: "Faith is that which gives coherence, integration, and in large measure strength to what may be described as ego or personality."[1] I understand trust as the ego solvent that dissolves and disrupts personality and destroys character. I am not interested in building character, but in destroying it. Jim is concerned with wholes. I am interested in holes, in the pigeon flying out of the pigeon hole. All of this is over-generalization, of course, but it is good to explore the extremes of our differences before we come to the middle ground of our similarities.

Jim's analysis underlines those aspects of faith that are moral, principled, responsible, and coherent. Faith development parallels the development of moral behavior. I am, like Friedrich Nietzsche, more mystic and less moral.[2] Trust is beyond good and evil. Religious intuition has very little to do with morality. Morality is largely culturally determined and must be transcended toward what Tillich called the development of a "trans-moral conscience."[3] Morality is the basis of our character armor.

I experience trust as a closer relative of sex and madness and mysticism than of morality. I am interested primarily in those experiences in which the individual is dissolved and has the sense that he is being moved by a power beyond himself. This is the experience Rudolf Otto described as the confrontation with the Holy.[4] The Holy Other breaks into and destroys the human categories of understanding, shattering the nice coherences we have managed to make. It fractures the intellect.

Jim is interested in faith as a centering principle. I am concerned with that basic trust that allows me to lose my integrity, to be a joyful fraction, to be eccentric, *not* to have my center in myself. In Nietzsche's terms, trust is the confidence that the center is everywhere. I focus on the pluralism that allows personality to disintegrate in a creative way, on the divine madness that allows us to lose ourselves.

By way of balance, I would like to recall something William James said in the *Sentiment of Rationality*.[5] Reason has two movements: It tries to unify, to embrace everything, to move toward monism, to create coherence. But it is also empirical and pluralistic, and investigates individuals. The bent of Jim's mind is toward the first mode of reason; my senses draw me toward the second.

A Definition of Trust

After this initial assault on the position of James-Fowler-as-Apollonian, I will now take a very Apollonian turn and offer a definition of trust:

> Trust is manifested in a gradual or sudden yielding of the illusion of control and a concomitant loss of character and transformation of personality.

I would like to tickle out this definition. For the once-born personality, trust is gradual. It is created by nurture. For the twice-born or conversionary personality, it is sudden. In either case, there is the yielding of the illusion of control. This includes intellectual controls and the effort to explain and understand everything. Trust involves transcendence of culture. It is primarily mystical. It is a category which is beyond the moral.

A good definition does more than say what something is. It also says what it is not. In my scheme the opposite of trust is paranoia or untrust. The paranoid is a special kind of monist. He really has it together. The whole world is his oyster, and like the guy in the Alka Seltzer commercial, he ate the whole thing and has a tremendous stomach ache—paranoid delusions.

Trusting and Untrusting Bodies:

A Carnal Approach to Sin and Salvation

How are trust and distrust manifest in the body? I start with an assumption that is fairly universal among religious folk: We are all sinners. The doctrine of original sin is perhaps the most empirical of all the religious doctrines. It can be translated by saying that we come into the world injured. There are no perfect specimens except in Platonic heavens or in typological constructs. We are all wounded. This means that we are all foreshortened. We are all contorted, all tortured characters. The clearest place to see our distortion is in the body and the body politic—not the mind. I am not trying to deny the mind in order to come to the senses, but I am interested in the relationship of the body to trust and untrust.

Let us translate the notion of sin and salvation into bodily terms. Our bodies, as well as our personalities, are twisted by the character armor we develop to protect ourselves against real and imagined threats. The idea comes from Wilhelm Reich.[6] Reich, who was a contemporary of Freud, did something very radical. When he talked about pathology, about the crippledness of human life, he insisted upon translating mental language into structural and physical language. What Luther called unfaith, and psychologists call paranoia, Reich termed body, or character, armor. He saw that any emotional or psychological injury was perpetuated in the body by chronic patterns of tension or chronic atonic patterns. The body, thus, becomes a system that incarnates stress and dis-ease. When we are injured, emotionally or physically, our bodies petrify to form defenses against the world.

A political analogy: Every human personality is directed by a personal Pentagon. Just as the energies of this country are invested in defensive operations (over one-third of our national budget is dedicated to wars—past, present, and future), so our bodies are bound by the defense mechanisms we have developed. In psychological terms, sin means that a major part of the energy within the personality is devoted to the creation and maintenance of defensive systems.

Let us picture how character armor operates. You have all seen a dog that was beaten as a puppy. Even if you try to be-friend him, he cringes and shrinks away. His body is perma-nently formed in a cringing stance, his tail permanently be-tween his legs. Even in situations where there is no realistic danger, he retains the stance of a beaten puppy. In a similar way, we can identify the timid or passively dependent per-sonality that always reacts to challenge by becoming small and clinging. Or take the opposite, the aggressive, hostile person. The model for this personality type, that is arche-typically American and male, is the baboon. When the baboon thinks any other animal is going to invade his terri-tory, he swells his chest and starts swaggering around making fierce faces and noises. Baboon behavior and personality are taught at West Point. But the armor is even more pervasive than this; it is the idealized American character set.

In order to feel this typical American variety of "sin" or

character armor, let's perform a little experiment. Sit the way mother told you to sit. Stop slouching! Sit up straight! The West Point posture! Back straight! Shoulders up! Chest out! Suck in that gut! If you are a woman, I want you to picture the Playmate of the Month. Her profile is 36-24-36. If you're male, I'd like you to picture Charles Bronson at West Point.

Now to the second part of the experiment. Do you really have that stomach in and back straight? First, notice the feeling in your anal sphincter. That is called being "up tight" or, in other circles, "tight-assed." The next thing to notice is your breathing. Be sure to keep your gut in. You have to have a wasp waist in WASP America. Structure your body *right*. Keep it in a straight line. Feel your breathing? Don't change it. Be aware of how you can breathe when you are in the ideal posture.

This is the "proper" American posture. It is recommended for the Playmate of the Month and the Marlboro Man. Notice the complete displacement of the personality. You are displacing energy up toward the head. An ideal of good posture, of how you should look, is determining how you hold your body.

Return to your breathing. You didn't slump did you? Notice that you are breathing in exaggerated short breaths. Notice also that you cannot feel anything below the waist. You have gone to sleep below the waist. There is a separation of genitals and heart. Your breathing patterns are appropriate to stress-type behavior. Anxiety is always correlated with rapid breathing patterns.

OK. Now let loose. So much for the ideal American character and posture. Let us talk about this a bit more and then we can turn to alternatives.

The displacement upward of the personality, where the ego and breath are forced up toward the head, is the typical problem in our culture. We are split between the head and the body. We construct magnificent monuments to that split, such as medical centers where psychiatrists and physicians work separately on the illnesses of body and mind. It is not surprising. All of Western culture has been split in body and mind since the time of Descartes.[7]

There is another aspect of Western culture that is embodied in this body-mind split. The mind is supposed to govern the body. The center of the personality is in the head. It is called "capitalism." Capital, you will remember, is merely the Latin word for "head." In a capitalized society, mind governs matter, capital governs labor, the head governs the body.

American capitalism and the Marlboro man personality it produces have a definite hierarchy of values. The highest value is assigned to mind, head, reason, control, rationality, technique—that is, to what traditionally have been the "masculine" virtues. The "feminine" virtues, which are associated with body knowledge, touch, emotion, surrender, and art, are less highly valued. Control is up. Being controlled is down. Head workers are more valuable than body workers. Management is the place to be. (Except that my electrician charges more than my psychiatrist, so there are exceptions!) To be "good" is to be male and all the other things that go with being male. White Anglo-Saxon males are better than other males. The worst thing to be is a black homosexual poet. Females, generally, are slightly less equal and less rational than men. You cannot trust people who have menstrual cycles to run for the presidency. There could be a crisis, and they might think with their hearts. These judgments and values are built into our national character armor. Obsession with control is built into Western personality and is manifest as paranoia. We distrust what we cannot control.

The typically American form of sin is related to this urge to control. It can be seen in the commercials for Preparation H. One symptom of the American way of sin, we're told, is that a third to one-half of Americans suffer from constipation and hemorrhoids. We are also told that salvation from this sin is Preparation H. It is typical of the American character that we believe in scientific nostrums. In reality, constipation and hemorrhoids are philosophical problems that science and medicine cannot solve. From childhood we are told that we must control ourselves. The head must control the body. The body must function regularly and follow orders. It must eliminate wastes once every twelve hours. To comply with our constipated need for control and order, to do our duty regularly, we push our bodies. We push until the pushing is translated into hemorrhoids. This is the model of unfaith, of untrust. Hemorrhoids, the national disease, is the sign of our paranoia or, in theological terms, of our untrust.

I used to be constipated until I was cured one day by one sentence in a book. The sentence that converted me was something like "There is no such thing as constipation." The book went on to explain peristaltic action. The body is constructed to take care of its own elimination needs. It does this on its own time schedule. Body time is what the ancient Greeks called *kairos*, a qualitative kind of time that awaits the significant moment for something to happen. In English, our word "timing" carries some of this meaning. But we try to control our bodies by the kind of time the Greeks called *chronos*, a quantitative kind of time that deals with the measurable aspect of the continuous flux. This kind of time is kept by watches and calendars, not bodies.

I will make a wild wager that 90 percent of the suffering in the hospitals around us comes from stress that is caused by a chronological view of history and the related view that human beings must control their world. Most stress is a result of the strategies, the pace, the foods, the drugs that we use in order to keep our bodies functioning in chronologically efficient patterns.

I am especially conscious of the widespread use of drugs when I travel. Since I am from California, when I fly East my body is still on California time. So I resort to drugs—coffee and sugar—to zip up my body, to get it working on *chronos* rather than *kairos*.

The fascinating book *Type "A" Behavior and Your Heart*[8] bears out the relationship between disease, stress, and chronological time. The authors contend that you cannot avoid a heart attack merely by changing your diet. You have to change your philosophy of life. The notion that we must control everything leads to paranoia and to the destruction of the body.

Untrust can destroy us. Our problem is character armor, the way we construct our bodies, our economic system, our ideological system, and our class system to maintain control of the world. The dominant problem of the human personality is our compulsion to control. We live by compulsions, to have power, to control, to make the world coherent and safe. This, then, is the problem, not the answer.

As an aside, Carlos Castaneda[9] is not the answer either. Philosophically, he is still a Western, male chauvinist. The dominant images he is concerned with are the "man of power" and "the warrior." It is the warrior in us and the man of power who refuse to believe the world is trustworthy. Once we make the assumption that we are only safe when we are in control, we structure all of our reality to prove we are right. Nothing that is out of control can be trusted. The national humiliation of Vietnam is the end result of a paranoid policy, of the effort to be warriors and men of power such as I am describing. Most disease is, like the Pentagon, a symptom of our paranoid way of dealing with the world. Most of the systems we construct, which make up culture, keep our boundaries well-defined and tight. In trust we must break through our compulsive rationality to find out what lies on the other side of our mistrust. We must break through these cultural systems to relate our own kyrological time to the rhythms of the body.

Let me say this in another way by talking about character armor and repression. The dominant repression in our culture is not sexual, as it was in Freud's time. Our society fears and represses religious intuition. You can talk about incest with your mother in educated society and nobody bats an eyelash, but if you talk about your deep-seated desire to believe in God, to believe that the universe is controlled by something other than human effort, that is very embarrassing.

I have embarrassed more than one therapist by insisting that I needed to deal with a religious problem. They begin to stutter, fidget, look away, and mutter. They do not know how to deal with the basic desire to believe that we do not need to control things. Yet the need to control everything is the root of paranoia. And grace happens in those moments when my controls are swept away or when I surrender and yield myself to a power beyond my control. The most usual settings in which this happens are in sex, work, meditation, and observing the small wonders of everyday life. It is the repression of mysticism, sexual ecstasy, and compassion that leads to the untrusting personality.

Let me be more specific about the untrusting or paranoid personality. This is found in the person who refuses to trust or who cannot trust and so centers the entire world around himself. The essence of a paranoid is that he has a very strong center. He has a center so strong that he cannot believe that any event is unconnected to him. If somebody whispers in the next booth in a Holiday Inn, he thinks they are talking about him. When the clerk laughs in a store, the paranoid says to himself, "They're laughing at me!" The whole world is completely organized for the paranoid. He has a technique and a system that allows him to be the center of everything. Unfortunately, everything is experienced as hostile.

Trust is the reverse of paranoia. To trust is to believe that in some unknown sense everything in the world is connected and benevolent. Everything is connected so that I am not the center of the world; therefore, I do not have to control it. I can let go.

The circle that began with my definition of faith as trusting has now come all the way around to the place where we started: Trust is manifested in a gradual or sudden yielding of the illusion of control and the concomitant loss of character and transformation of personality. What this means experientially is that the more I trust, the less I have to tie everything together. Trust allows me to tolerate plurality in the body and the body politic. Emotionally, it means I do not have to be consistent. I can contain many contradictions.

I used to be a very consistent person. Now, on a good day, I range from suicidal despair to ecstatic hope, from anger and aggression to surrender and trust. I define a good day as one on which I am able to use my entire emotional range. Earlier in my life I had a very limited emotional range because I did not trust myself to have emotions.

To feel is to be in contradiction. When there are no contradictions there are no feelings. This is why the image of the faithful person as the unified person is to me such a terrible image. Somebody asked me how I liked Zen. My answer was: if you like hardboiled eggs, you will love Zen. I love hardboiled eggs at a picnic, but only one egg. Hardboiled eggs without pickles and without spice and all the other things that go with them are not my idea of a feast.

Trusting: Life After Forty

I would like to get confessional and say plainly how I feel about trusting. As I understand the second part of life, my task is to destroy what I built in the first part of my life. At about the age of forty, I began to be very tired of being Sam Keen. All the character armor I had built up in the first part of my life—the modes of coping, the intellectual way of unifying and ordering the world, my defense system—began to crumble. The second part of my life appears radically discontinuous with the first part of my life. I no longer know where I am going. I do not have organized futures. I cannot control things. Now I experience life as much more benevolent. The less I control and the less I order, the more certain I am that there is already an ordering principle built into the universe.

What bothers me most about Jim's model is that it is subtly gnostic. It glorifies the man of knowledge rather than the man of trust and the man of compassion. In the Biblical tradition, trust is a virtue of those who are blind, not of those who are enlightened. Trust is in God and not in a human being's ability to make cognitive sense out of the world. The real key to understanding is—(pencils ready?): There is no key to understanding everything! Trust is the increasing ability to live in a world that I do not have to understand, that I do not have to control, that I do not have to order cognitively. Trust means getting on the other side of personality, getting on the other side of character.

The character that grew in the first part of my life was largely made by my parents, my culture, and myself. I was masculine. I could do a hundred sit-ups. I could not get a coat to fit me because I had forty-two-inch shoulders and a twenty-eight-inch waist. I was organized upward, toward the head. I have seen that Sam Keen disintegrate. I have come to see things in a different way. In Jungian terms,[10] I have had to get in touch with sensation, feeling, and intuition. I have had to learn to love disorder.

Learning to trust involves integrating the opposites. For men it means learning to surrender to the feminine. For women it means becoming warriors. Women are well-advised to quit surrendering, and to seize a portion of the world and order it. Do exactly what Jim Fowler talks about in his faithing model. His advice is good for women. Ordering is the neglected side of their personality. For men I think it is terrible advice.

One of the interesting things about universities and bureaucracies is that they have been dominated by an untrusting form of thinking. The types who are rewarded are the knower, the warrior, and the controller. About the time most men become successful they begin to disintegrate. They want something more than power or knowledge. The character traits which insured success in the corporation or the university are antithetical to those needed to live the second half of life in a vivid way. What happens when character armor begins to soften? Suddenly, instead of being in touch with the impulse to order, you get in touch with dreams, imagery, sensation, and intuition. Professionally, this may be very disturbing. It can lead to the loss of tenure. Your values become different. You no longer want what you wanted before.

Once character defenses are surrendered and replaced by trust, there is a new birth—a new person emerges. Novelty enters history. If we speak of grace we affirm at the same time that we are radically free. We are not culturally bound creatures. We are in culture, but there is something in us that transcends culture. Our freedom allows us to erase our cultural conditioning in some significant measure. This principle of novelty accounts for the revolutions both in per-

Table 2.1

Child	PERIOD OF CONSTRUCTION OF CHARACTER—PERSONALITY

In Freudian terms: Oral
Dependent
Primary Word: Yes
Life Stance: I am *with* you
Task: Develop basic trust, harmony
Pathology: One arrested in this stage remains passively dependent
   and does not emerge from imbeddedness in the matrix

Rebel

In Freudian terms: Anal
Counter-dependent
Primary Word: No
Life Stance: I am *against* you
Task: Develop ability to doubt, to criticize, to be alienated, to
   resist exterior authority
Model: The Warrior. The Rebel. Prometheus. Adam.
Pathology: One arrested in this stage becomes alienated within a
   negative identity, paranoid.

Adult	CONSTRUCTION OF CHARACTER ARMOR

In Freudian terms: Genital
Inter-dependent
Yes and No
Life Stance: Coping
Task: Build self-confidence, self-esteem, a strong ego. Become
   normal and satisfied and adjusted. Cooperation.
Model: The Worker. The Citizen.

Virtues: The Scout law. Pledge of Allegiance to cultural institutions.
Pathology: Average person is arrested here. Outcome is one-dimensional person, eventually boredom and despair. The limit of the once-born personality. Life is finished at 40.

Outlaw   *DESTRUCTION OF CHARACTER ARMOR*

Post-Freudian: The Erotic Person
True Independence: Autonomy
Life Stance: Exploring the limits of the self. Transcending. The path of desire.
Model: The Hero. The Shaman. The Adventurer. The Mystic. The supra-normal person who goes "beyond good and evil" into divine madness which exists on the far side of personality.
Pathology: If arrested here the individual becomes alienated in arrogance and hubris and is cut off from community. Power but no love.

Lover and Fool   *LIFE BEYOND CHARACTER*

Second Innocence: The childlike Sage
Compassion: Theonomy
Life Stance: Openness. Unself-consciousness. A cosmopolitan lover who is without "character" and therefore responsive to cosmos—polis and eros. The lover lives in *kairos* and *chronos.* Silence and laughter are characteristic.
Model: The Knight of Faith. The Enlightened Person. The Saint. The person with no-self who is beyond intra-psychic conflict.
Pathology: None (except drugs may give a premature sense of this stage and give the young the illusion that they have arrived before they have begun).

---

sonality and the body politic. This principle is at the center of what I mean by "trust." Trust is the ability to allow novelty.

Character armor is always conspiring to rule out novelty, to prevent the unexpected from happening. The more I get in touch with the part of my personality that surprises me, with dreams and the unconscious, the more I am impressed with the principle of grace within myself. The problem of religious education is not how to write religious answers on the tablets of the mind but how to erase the false religion and false values our culture has programmed into us.

Stages on Life's Way

I would like to offer a systematic outline of my notion of the path of life, of the stages in the development of the fullest kind of human life.

For the most part, Chart 3.1 is self-explanatory so I will only make random comments. I would like to emphasize that there is nothing automatic about the development of these stages. In fact, I suspect that few people get beyond the third stage of adulthood and fewer yet get to the fifth stage of the lover. It might be better to call these *dimensions* of life rather than stages. All the earlier stages remain in the person who advances to the later stages and the later dimensions are present in promise, even in those persons who psychologically never leave childhood or rebellion.

The Child. The essence of the child is dependency. The primary task early in life is learning to be *with* others. The mark of a successful child is the ability to say "Yes." When children conform, adults say, "That's a good child." This is what the child hears, so the first thing the child becomes concerned with is being "good." The child intuits the values of the parents, constructs a superego, and accepts what the culture values. This is the first stage of acculturation. It is what Jim Fowler calls the Intuitive-Projective Stage. It is preoperational, prelinguistic and presymbolic. Trust is mediated by the hands, by the way a child is held and is allowed to be held by others.

The Rebel. The rebel is exactly the opposite of the child. The rebel is counterdependent. S/he is primarily *against.* His/her primary word is "No." If mother says, "Do you want chocolate chip cookies?" s/he is likely to say "No." This stage begins with the "terrible twos."

The rebel is defining him/herself against others. S/he is against what the parents describe as good and what the culture describes as good. Doubt, resistance, and rebellion are virtues in the stage of life when one is discovering an identity that is distinct from the parents. However, when rebellion hardens into a way of life, the rebel becomes a paranoiac, a warrior, an alienated individual.

The Adult. I do not think the adult can be said to be genuinely independent. S/he can say both "Yes and No." S/he knows both the good and the evil of the culture. S/he can be with, against, and to some extent independent of others, but his/her dominant virtue is cooperation. An adult has developed the ego strength to assume and perform social roles: husband, worker, wife, citizen, consumer.

At this point in life there is a dividing line. The truly independent person is supranormal, a postadult. Only a few, an elite company of heroes and heroines, develop the courage and trust necessary to take the journey to the far side of character. It takes an abnormal amount of trust to go beyond the culture's crust.

During the first part of life there is an increasing accumulation of character. A successful adult is one whose character is established. As children we had little character armor. But by the time we become successful adults, we must affirm the values of the culture. A convenient summary of American adulthood is found in the Boy Scout law: "A Scout is trustworthy, loyal, helpful, friendly, courteous, kind, obedient, cheerful, thrifty, brave, clean and reverent." "On my honor I will do my best to do my duty to God and my country, to obey the Scout Law, to respect other people at all times, and to take cold showers. . . ."

I am not clear how much disagreement Jim Fowler and I have about the stages beyond adulthood. We use different symbols and have a different style of expression, but I hear him talking about the necessity to go beyond culture. When I talk about going beyond the crust of culture, I am referring to moving from being the Adult to being the Outlaw.

The Outlaw. The Outlaw stage begins with a crime, the killing of the old authorities. It is the story of Adam and Eve and of Prometheus and of every person who decides to find out what life in the wild is all about. The path starts where conscience (Freud—the watching institution, the superego, the internalized voice of the culture) is violated and one dares to live without the sanction of the authorities in the land "beyond good and evil."

The outlaw quests for autonomy. S/he wants to discover the depths of the self that lie beneath the roles and duties that have governed the adult. After half a lifetime of conforming and coping, the fledgling outlaw is animated by a desire to explore the plurality, the madness, the uncontrolled forces that have previously been held in check by the character armor. Since the outlaw must find his/her way through a forest of false desires to discover the true desires of the deepest self, s/he must pass through a period of intense self-consciousness, experimentation, and disillusionment. All of the old values must be questioned. The terror of the void, the demons of doubt, despair, and death must be faced. The price of self-knowledge is high. Its reward is higher.

The normal adult is shocked by the selfishness of the outlaw. What right has any person to make the question, "What do I *really* desire?" the guiding question. Religious adults, in particular, seem threatened by the outlaw. All institutions prefer that the moral question, "What *ought* I to do?" be the guiding question. The authoritarian personality agrees with Kant that there is a necessary conflict between morality and desire and that a good person is one who puts duty before inclination.[11] Strangely, neither Kant nor Christian ethicists have paid much attention to one of the fundamental insights of the Christian tradition: love is prior to law. Augustine said, *"Dilige et quod vis, fac"* (Love—esteem highly—and do what you will).[12] The path of love takes us to God. Grace is prior to morality. The outlaw dares to question the cultural wisdom that says we cannot at once be full of pleasure and full of goodness. The theology of Augustine implies that if we follow the path of the deepest pleasure we will find the most sacred manner of life.

The paradox is that by following the path of individual desire the outlaw is brought face to face with the need for communion. The deepest pleasure is always shared. Satisfaction is a community affair. The sex act is a paradigm. The most ecstatic pleasures result from two persons sharing the deepest and widest range of their individual passions. Don Juan knew very little about pleasure because he was not concerned with the fullness of his partner. Sex at best is communication, communion, community. The deepest desire of the individual is to lose his/her individuality in the dance of life. Ecstasy is being-with.

There is great danger connected with the path of the outlaw. Kierkegaard wrestled with the problem of "the teleological suspension of the ethical" in the story of Abraham and Isaac.[13] Every individual who puts him/herself above the dictates of the community is prey to the dangers of demonic inflation. Prophets, sibyls, mystics, and mass killers—sacred and demonic madmen/women—all transcend the normal requirements of morality. The outlaw easily slips into being the amoral criminal or the visionary sociopath if s/he loses touch with the simple pleasures—the touch of flesh, the comfort of the hearth, the smell of earth, the talk of friends. Friendship is one of the strongest antidotes to demonic inflation. Finally, the outlaw must confront the phenomenon that brings him/her back to the community of ordinary mortals: death. It may be that meditation on death brings the profound sense of mortality and humility that marks the passage from the outlaw to the lover.

The Lover or the Fool. This last stage of my model is roughly equivalent to Fowler's universalizing stage. I am reluctant to speak too much about it for two reasons. Most of my knowledge of this stage comes from hearsay. I am more of an outlaw than a lover. I hope to travel closer to this land of unity and homecoming, but as yet I still live in the plurality and chaos of the outlaw territory. There is also an ancient tradition that the true lover cannot communicate the knowledge of the unity of things in any direct language. "Those who know don't tell; those who tell don't know." The enlightened man or woman coming back from nirvana has nothing to say. The world is no different. It is still *samsara,* a place of suffering and conflict. But s/he sees it differently. The conflict is now experienced as the agony of a divine game rather than as ultimate tragedy. In psychology, descriptions of pathology are always more elaborate than descriptions of health. Neurosis is dramatic; health is calm. For the lover, the world has ceased to be a problem to be solved and has become a mystery to be enjoyed.

The clue to the personality of the lover is that vulnerability and compassion have replaced defensiveness and paranoia. The lover has come back to the basic trust of the child. S/he is primarily *with*. The vision of second innocence turns the world from a battleground into an arena where divine forces are playing out a love drama. The seeming plurality of things only masks a deeper unity. The communion of all beings is the hidden truth. The lover can say "all is one" and know what s/he is talking about. It is only after the tragedy of disease, evil, and death has been wrestled with that authentic love begins to emerge. I suspect the "wisdom" of twenty-year-old children who have had no encounter with the raw side of life. When they say "All is one," they don't know what they are talking about. Psychedelic drugs, which can give a vision of the territory inhabited by the lover, often seduce the young into premature peace. You cannot lose an ego that you have not constructed. Character armor must be built before it can be destroyed. *Karma* must be accumulated before it can be burnt. The whole notion of teaching young people to be saints before they have been sinners is ridiculous. The yogis and spiritual masters who advocate wall-to-wall spiritual disciplines for adolescents have no respect for the wisdom of time. They try to teach wisdom before folly has been tasted. They train children to give Sunday school affirmations of love before they have discovered the depths of their untrust.

The lover is animated by a life that is deeper than the ego or personality. In traditional terms, s/he is moved by grace. The spontaneity and unself-consciousness of the lover is in marked contrast to the experimental self-consciousness of the outlaw. The lover has ceased to be concerned with the question "Who am I?" and has been invaded by a conviction that we are all one.

The lover is also a fool because s/he can look at the tragedy of history and say: "Nevertheless . . . I trust." S/he looks at death but can still affirm that death is not the final fact about the cosmos. When the fool recovers the second innocence of the child, both the past and the future open wide. Time becomes an open story. Memory and hope grow strong and mingle to create a person who is almost infinitely open to the infinity of the present moment.

Perhaps the lover or the fool is an ideal that can never be fully actualized, an impossible possibility that sleeps within our depths. I cannot speak about the limits of this way of being in the world with any authority. The vision is compelling. I would like to become a lover, but at this stage in my life I am still hampered by fears of losing my individuality and by the lurking presence of death. I suspect, but I do not know firsthand, that true lovers have digested the fear of death and transformed it into a bold spontaneity.

The Marshmallow Demons and the Fire Demons

I would like to close this presentation by emphasizing a certain balance that might easily be overlooked in my rather polemical style.

The problem of thinking in terms of Apollo and Dionysus is that the Greek plays about Dionysus were written by Apollonians. And Apollonians are always terrified by what might happen if we really did let loose. They fear license, excess, the tearing and eating of flesh. Their fear is that if we had emotional freedom, it would lead to uncorseted excess. This is not true.

There is an old Buddhist legend in which someone asks about freedom and discipline. The Buddha says to a woman, "What would you call a hand which is clenched into a tight fist?"

"I would call that distorted," the woman replied. "Any hand clenched like that all the time is certainly crippled."

The Buddha then asked, "What would you call a hand that is always loose, limp and hanging?" The woman had to answer the last question in the same way: "Such a hand that is always limp is also distorted. It too is crippled."

What we want, then, is neither a body that has no tension nor a body that is filled with tension. We want a body that can flow but which can be tensile. A lover or a fool does not cease being a warrior. But he or she ceases being a warrior all the time.

There are two kinds of demons in our culture that plague us. They are the marshmallow demons and the fire demons. The Pentagon and what it represents are the fire demons and those who brought flowers to encircle the Pentagon were the marshmallow demons. If you have ever danced with a hippie, you know what I mean. It is like dancing with a marshmallow —no bones, just "Let it all flow, baby." We need both fierceness and tenderness, both discipline and love, both moderation and excess.

My closing point is this: we are all androgynous, all male and female. We are all Apollo and Dionysus, but this is only true when we can get to the point of surrender and can say, "Here I am. Let it happen." We need to be outraged at a predatory world. We need to battle social evil but not to project it outward. Vietnam is not something *they* did. It is something *we* did. We all laid waste the children. This includes the

Vietcong. We *all* did it. It is necessary to remain in touch with the murderous parts of ourselves.

There is a paradox in being androgynous, in realizing our capacity for love and evil, for male and female, for Apollo and Dionysus. If we see our capacity to be cruel, we may also begin to understand our ability to be loving and nurturing.

References:*   Second Presentation

1. James W. Fowler, "Faith Development: Theory and Research," Unpublished manuscript furnished to Keen for the Colloquium, Chap. 2, p. 1.

2. Friedrich Wilhelm Nietzsche, *Beyond Good and Evil*, in *Basic Writings of Friedrich Nietzsche* (Westminister, Maryland: Modern Library Giants, 1900). First published in 1886 as *Jenseits von Gut und Bose.* Nietzsche advocates moving beyond the master morality and slave morality to the *Ubermensch*, one who transcends him or herself somewhat like a "Roman Caesar with Christ's soul." (Master morality makes independence, generosity, self-reliance, etc. virtues, while slave morality sees the good as reticence and all that diminishes suffering and striving.) Nietzsche also spoke against the "English psychologists" who saw good only in what was socially useful. Of the utilitarians, he says: "Those men are simply dull old frogs."

3. Paul Tillich, *Morality and Beyond* (New York: Harper Torchbook, 1963), pp. 65-81. Tillich defines the trans-moral conscience as one that ". . . judges not in obedience to a moral law, but according to its participation in a reality that transcends the sphere of moral commands. A trans-moral conscience does not deny the moral realm, but is driven beyond it by the unbearable tensions of the sphere of the law." See p. 77.

4. Rudolf Otto, *The Idea of the Holy* (New York: Oxford University Press, 1958). First translated into English in 1923 from *Das Heilige* (1917). This book investigates the "non-rational element in the idea of the divine," although that element need not be considered counter to reason. The Holy is an irreducible quality which is called "numinous" by Otto from the Latin word *numen.* The numinous is a mysterious, awe-inspiring, and terrible (*mysterium tremendum et fascinans*) deity which is apprehended by humankind's religious faculty.

5. William James, "Sentiment of Rationality," in *The Will to Believe, Human Immortality and Other Essays on Popular Philosophy* (New York: Dover Publications, 1956), pp. 63-110. First published in 1896.

*Ed.

6. Wilhelm Reich, *Character Analysis* (New York: A Touchstone Book, Simon and Schuster, 1945).

7. Descartes (1596-1650) reduced the world of matter to the primary quality of extension in space. In addition to "extended substance," there was also "thinking substance" to be accounted for. This he discovered by the application of critical doubt to the point that the only thing not doubted was that he was doubting. "Thinking substance" was independent from all natural substances, even the body. See especially his *Discourse on Method* (1637).

8. Meyer Friedman and Ray H. Rosenman, *Type "A" Behavior and Your Heart* (New York: Knopf, 1974).

9. Carlos Castaneda, *The Teachings of Don Juan, A Separate Reality,* and *Journey to Ixtlan* (New York: Simon and Schuster, 1974).

10. Carl G. Jung, *Psychological Types*, Bollingen Series 20 (Princeton, N.J.: Princeton University Press, 1971). First published in 1920. Jung's "four functional types" describe the means by which the consciousness orients to experience. We tend to prefer different means of perception and evaluation. *Sensation* (sense perception) tells us that something is. *Thinking* tells us what it is that we experience. *Feeling* tells us whether it is agreeable to us or not. *Intuition* tells us by guess or hunch where the experience comes from and where it is going.

11. Immanuel Kant (1724-1804) said that since we cannot always choose our inclinations of a physical or psychological nature, we must do our duty in the ethical situation. Duty presents itself when one can universalize it or make it into a universal law or a law of nature. Kant's categorical imperative is not hypothetical. One does it for itself and not because of any feelings or consequences. See especially his *Critique of Practical Reason* and *Metaphysics of Morals*.

12. Augustine, *Ep. Joan*, vii, 5, in J. P. Migne, *Patralogiae cursus completus* series Latina (Paris: Garnier Fr., 1864), Vol. 35, col. 2033. The context for this famous phrase is: *Semel ergo breve praeciptum tibi praecipitur, Dilige, et quod vis fac.* It is not *Ama et fac quod vis* (Love with desire and do what you please), as it is often rendered. Keen is suggesting that love use laws as a means rather than as an end. He is not saying that all law should be done away with.

13. Soren Kierkegaard, *Either/Or*, 2 vols., trans. W. Lowrie (Princeton, N.J.: Princeton University Press, 1971). The stages on life's way for Kierkegaard are: the esthetic, the ethical, and the religious. The goal of the esthetic life is one's satisfaction, while the goal of the ethical

life is performing one's duty. The goal of the religious life is being an individual before God. Development is not continuous and each stage has its own criteria to evaluate the other stages. The criterionless choice is either/or. There is no gradual ladder of reason to climb. One must make a "leap of faith."

The example of Abraham and Isaac illustrates how the religious life is reduced to either doing what God commands or not. The command to kill one's son is against inclination (esthetic view) and is murder (ethical view). It makes no sense outside the context of the religious stage where one is before God and aided by God's creative act. It is in this situation that one suspends both the ethical and the esthetic inclinations to do what God commands.

Dialogue: Jim Fowler* and Sam Keen*

Crossing Boundaries

The Setting

The Institute of Religion Building is a four story structure in the middle of the Texas Medical Center complex. From the second story windows of Dawson Bryan Hall one sees hospitals, medical schools, research institutions, schools of nursing, a dental school and other health care facilities.

Following the morning presentations, first by Fowler and then by Keen, the second floor of the Institute was filled with the aroma of French cooking at its simple best. The flavor of a country inn sent people chattering into seminar rooms, the sitting room, and all about Dawson Bryan Hall to savor food, drink and talk. Celebration began to catch up with inquiry.

After the last pastry was gone and the plates and glasses cleared away, the afternoon began. The stiffness of the morning had softened and people sat together. The issues no longer seemed to be a matter of clash between two personalities. The prize, sought in common, lay far beyond that room.

One Spring Day

In the dialogue, Jim spoke first and then Sam answered. They were soon speaking together. The text of the dialogue has been left as it was with a minimum of editing.

All notes are the author's unless otherwise indicated.

James Fowler: Legend tells us that when the unicorn wounds with its single horn it also heals as it wounds. In a sense, Sam Keen has been unicornlike in his wounding of me and my point of view. The wounds have not been lethal. They have been opening and they do give me a chance to heal, and with him, too, perhaps. I appreciate what you have done, Sam.

I think you are right to say that there is a fundamental stylistic difference in the directions we are coming from. I am prepared to play "Apollo" in our discussion and to be the "heavy." I am prepared to be the foil for Dionysus. On the other hand, I have found the introduction to your book, *Voices and Visions*, which contains your *Psychology Today* interviews, to be an awful (in the good sense of being full of awe) Apollonian way of reflecting on your Dionysian experiences. You own up to that, too, I know, and you have said so.

What I would like to do now is to pick up some of the ideas touched on in our thrusting about. I would like to clarify some of the unicornlike wounds and also counter some of the thrusts that have come my way. It is a clarifying and healing as well as a countering task that I have in mind now as we continue on our journey.

Centering and Decentering

James Fowler: One of the things that I have tried to communicate about the developmental schema I have been using is that we have noticed evidence of both centering and decentering going on simultaneously. It seems to me that this double dynamic parallels closely what you are talking about here, Sam. The person who can see the unity of all the fantastic plurality out there in the world is a person who has a nonegocentric unity.

Your outlaw gives the world unity, but he is not paranoid. He insists upon himself and says to culture that it cannot define him. It cannot put him under "oughts." Your outlaw is one who can say that he is in that position and is entitled to follow his wants.

He is a little like the rebel you described in not seeking complementarity with the cosmos. He is asserting his program over against the cosmos, and yet he is not paranoid to the point of closing out the cosmos.

Sam Keen: It is true that the outlaw goes back to the self, because the self is the source of knowledge.

When I reached forty years of age, I finally realized how my mind had been programmed by the culture. Everybody told me what was good and proper and patriotic. I finally had to wipe the slate and start again in small ways. Father Lynch speaks of this in his book, *Images of Hope.*[1] He noticed that people in mental institutions began to heal when they started to ask to have their wants met. They began small. "Do I want coffee or do I want tea? What *do* I want? I want tea." I had to return to my wants. I discovered, for example, that I wanted communication with other people. I wanted community. But *I* wanted it. The process of being honest about our desires leads to the development of what Eastern philosophies called the true "witness-self" or what Christians term the Holy Spirit. There is a transcendental point of perspective on myself that is necessary to live beyond the adult stage.

I discovered the transcendental perspective of the outlaw when I was living in an apartment by myself in a strange city without a job. I had lost both my family and my lover. Every morning I awoke, looked at the bare walls and asked, "What do I want to do today?" The room was shimmering with a kind of craziness. Finally, I began to meditate. I sat, just sat, and watched. Watching, I discovered that I could go up above a hundred feet or more and look down at old Sam Keen. I could watch him go through all those tape loops that made up his personality. Gradually I developed a compassionate, objective perspective toward my own follies. I began to become an outlaw. I observed and began to alter the laws that had previously governed my psyche. By stepping into the calm observatory, I discovered in meditation that I could transcend my "personality" and laugh at myself. So, I don't think of the outlaw as being egocentric. He has gotten out of the ego, and has begun to find the self.

Fowler: This seems to be an illustration of what I am trying to talk about with regard to the second naivete.* It is the development of the capacity to see the self and let the self be. All that armor-building prior to that stage, though, is what made both the possibility and the necessity of going beyond one's armor for growth.

We need to be very careful in describing this process, however. We need to point out the discontinuities, but we also need to make clear the tremendous continuities. This is the heart of the whole idea of stage development. The outlaw and the break with the armor of the adult and conventionality, the break with what is in one's guts, as you put it, is a break that requires all the tools that one has acquired in the construction process.

A person in development needs certain tools and needs to surrender them when they are no longer useful. Development involves acquiring tools, using them, surrendering them, and repossessing them without being possessed by them.

Fowler refers to the "Role of Symbols" aspect of his Stage 5.— Ed.

Keen: There is something impetuous and adolescent about the outlaw in his or her search for self-knowledge, but this is very different from the rebel. The outlaw trembles with uncertainty but draws on the power s/he has accumulated by suffering the successes and disillusionments of adult life. The psychic cost of moving from adult to outlaw is much greater than the transition from rebel to adult. At eighteen the world is an oyster; at forty it has begun to clam up. It takes immense courage and energy to open it up again and turn it all into clam chowder.

Fowler: Let me try to clarify centering and decentering. You have pushed the notion of centering to the limits. You have said that the optimally centered person is a paranoiac who sees the whole world as rotating around himself or herself. I'd like to say that developmentally speaking the paranoid is a regressed, egocentric individual. He or she is very much like our Stage 1 child, in the sense of being unable to take the role of anyone else. This person is *literally* egocentric. The world literally centers around him or her, and there is no way to understand anyone else's perspective except to draw it into one's own perspective.

What I am talking about is both a centering and a series of recenterings, but it is also a decentering. It is the admitting of a wider and wider reality. I think that the kind of centering that I am speaking about grows more flexible, is more porous to experience and change as it grows. Its structure, therefore, is more differentiated and more adequate as well as more flexible.

Figure 3.1

There is a centering and a decentering that goes on simultaneously in faith development. If you take an image of two cones, as pictured in Figure 4.1, you might have some sense of the double direction of this centering and decentering. At the top point you have a self that is sure of itself, comfortable with itself, but is ready to release the boundaries of itself and be in mutuality with a commonwealth of being.

The role-taking column in my faith development chart deals with our successive abilities as human beings to take the roles of a wider and wider group of companions (represented by the inverted cone):

1. Rudimentary empathy
2. Simple perspective-taking
3. Mutual role-taking (interpersonal)
4. Mutual with self-selected group or class
5. Mutual with groups, classes, and traditions other than one's own
6. Mutual with the commonwealth of being

This is our attempt to put ourselves in someone else's position. It is our attempt to experience the world as they experience it. It is our way to enter their history and to understand why things look to them as they do, as well as to see the way they look to us.

You can now see that I am referring to a centering as well as to a decentering of the personality as one's faithing develops. This is why, Sam, I reject your characterization of my position as one which describes a paranoidal centering.

Apollonian Theory-Making is Dionysian in Fact

Fowler: I was anticipating the critique that this theory of faith development that I am proposing is all extremely cognitive. I was expecting to be called to task for making it extremely intellectual, all extremely up here in the head.

I am prepared to grant, I suppose, that the act of theory-making itself is an Apollonian kind of concern. I am also going to assert, however, that there is a very playful, almost Dionysian wildness about this kind of effort to conceive the thing as a whole.

One is reminded of Erik Erikson's comment. He once said that we have to take our heuristic models with a kind of serious playfulness and a playful seriousness.[2] There is a seriousness about this theory-making. There is a lot at stake in how you define normatively what it means to develop. It is playful in the sense that reality as we experience it always spills over the buckets in which we try to catch it. Part of the self-criticism in which I am engaged is an effort to be clear in my own mind where our buckets catch and hold truth and where truth spills over, or is ignored, or is not caught at all.

Two Kinds of Unconscious

Fowler: One of the areas, I think, that we need to talk about is the relationship between the kind of unconscious that this stage theory deals with and the kind that it does not. The structures I am trying to describe are unconscious. We are not generally aware of the "how" of our faithing.

We try to be aware of the content of our faithing though the structure remains unconscious. The content is what our beliefs and our rituals are about. We are not self-conscious about the structures underlying that or the processes by which we create and construct a world.

The unconscious structure of faith is different in kind from the dynamic unconscious. The dynamic unconscious is where we carry the psychic wounds, the deep longings, instinct, the hurts and fears. It carries the anxieties. These are the elements that emerge in dreams, in therapy, and sometimes in contemplation.

Perhaps if I had picked up the Eriksonian side of this and tried to talk about the way the successive integrations described in these stages incorporate psychodynamic gains, then the way I see the correlations here would be more adequately understood.

Let me give you a hint of what I mean. I think that our transition from Stage 4 to 5, which parallels Sam Keen's Outlaw Stage (and in interesting ways my 4 and 5 include the Outlaw Stage, it seems), involves the embrace of one's shadow and the animus and anima combination of C. G. Jung. I think it is important to correlate what I am able to describe with what Jung, Reich, and others, such as Erikson, have found.

While the theory I am using to describe reality is an Apollonian enterprise, in a partial sense it is not. As I tried to say earlier, faith is not a purely cognitive matter. I do not buy Jean Piaget's separation of cognition and affection. He would say that cognition is the structuring of knowing and that affection is the energetics, or that which moves or motivates the knowing.

A separation of faith-knowing into cognitive and affective aspects is a vestige of Cartesian epistemology that will not work. Augustine knew better. St. Paul knew better. A great many theologians have always known better. They have always known that faith involves *valuing*. It involves resting one's heart upon something, trusting someone, committing oneself to someone or something.

I argue that the stages I have described here in abstract language are not in themselves abstract at all. When you fill these structures with human experience, you see how knowing and valuing, fearing and trusting are all bundled up together in this enterprise.

Stage Transition and Pain

Fowler: If you follow me in my contention that the stages which I describe are structural wholes, or ways of constructing a world, then you can imagine what it is like to move from one stage to another. In rare instances it is a smooth, gradual, incremental transformation. In most cases stage transition comes with pain. It involves enduring the dissolution of your world. You must be able to endure the falling apart of that which is held together.

If this is a theory concerned about centering, it is also a theory that puts a heavy amount of emphasis upon the de-centering and disintegration that are necessary for a new creation.

In entering a new stage there is often the experience of a dark night of the soul. There is a time when God is the abyss, the void, or the enemy. The structure may be unconscious, but the experience of that transition is very much conscious and most often painful.

Trust and the Kinds of Knowing

Fowler: Some people say that trust is for the blind. I say that there are a lot of ways to be "blind." This was especially brought home to me during the taxi-ride conversation already mentioned with the playwright/divorce lawyer. He also asked, "What is it that keeps you working? It looks to me as if you're dealing in an area in which you can never know anything." He was referring to theology.

My reply was, "There are lots of ways to not be able to

know. There is a kind of not being able to know that says, I cannot know but somebody else can know. There is another way of not knowing. It says, I can know and others can know, but I don't know yet. In that case, you have to decide whether you want to or should know. A third kind of not knowing is where you don't know and no one else knows, so we are all equally lost, or blind. A final way of not knowing is to recognize that that which is most essential knowledge for our lives comes only with the investment of trust and commitment. Faith knows it cannot know God with the precision that we know physical objects. But our valuing, our purpose, our grasp of life's meaningfulness depend upon this more risky but essential knowing. That is faith.

I do not think that this theory of faith development describes a way of knowing in the positivist epistemological sense of grasping and pinning down. It is not analyzing and controlling. The knowing of faith is more like the second naivete that I have talked about. It is trusting. It is a knowing that has a mutuality. It is a knowing that has complementarity with the power that unifies our experience.

In this theory of faith development, each stage represents a kind of consciousness or knowing that is working toward a relationship of mutuality with the cosmos. What this theory shows is a series of transformations in that effort.

Sometimes the effort to create a mutuality with the cosmos involves pitting yourself against those who are trying to mediate that relationship for you. You have to say, "I must do it myself, or I can't do it at all." At other times it involves floating on what the tradition has offered you in the way of distilled wisdom in its symbols. You let those sustain you. You allow yourself to float there.

Love and Kohlberg's Stages of Moral Reasoning

Fowler: Sam Keen's point about "Love God and do what you will" and his affirmation of love as prior to morality caused me to reflect on Larry Kohlberg's schema for the development of moral reasoning. It seems to me that what you find in Kohlberg's work is the astute perception of our beginnings as premoral. We begin with "I want." After our beginning, we ascend through a second stage where we say, "I want, but other people are in the way." They have to be taken into account, so I have to want skillfully. It is only love that makes me begin to be moral at all. I love. I care about that other person. I care about that person's expectations of me. I don't want to disappoint that other person. Therefore, I begin to regard people as persons whose wants count as mine count. It is in this sense that love is the beginning of morality. (This is Kohlberg's Stage 3.)

When you reach the point where interpersonal love will not reconcile your wants with those of others, you get law (Stage 4). The next stage is when you find that law sometimes does as much injustice as justice. Love requires, then, moving beyond the law (Kohlberg's Stage 5 and 6).

How do you move beyond the law? You carry love (and I mean love in the hard sense and not the soft sentimental sense) toward others and caring toward others, even to anonymous others. Moral imagination becomes involved.

Love does not allow a return to your wants or merely to trying to find mutuality between your wants and those of others. It moves toward asking how you can make room for your wants as well as for the legitimate wants of others. How are you going to reconcile all this? Love takes form in justice.

Reclaiming the Body and the Body Politic

Fowler: There is a unicorn stab I have for Sam. It involves his talk about the body and the body politic. It seems to me that he should tell us how this sort of transformation of personality he is talking about avoids being merely an adjustment for a privileged few. How does it keep from being an adjustment for a privileged few to what are otherwise intolerable circumstances for the large majority of the people?

We need to know what the connection is between the transformation of persons, including the reclamation of the body, and the transformation of the body politic. This is what worries me most about Sam's theory and about mine.

I am afraid that our final stages, your Outlaw or Lover and my Stage 5 or 6, are too easily assimilated to our notion that faith is only an intrapsychic matter. There is a tendency to feel that if I can get myself straight, then society can go to hell, or take care of itself, or whatever. I think you have an answer to that, but it worries me.

Elites, Gifts, and the Body Politic

Keen: I agree with most everything you said up until your last comment, implying that in my view there might not be a link between the reclamation of the body and the transformation of the body politic. I would like to make my thinking about that link and about elites more explicit. The point you raise is crucial.

In the first place, I think that any developmental theory implies an elitism. It implies an evaluation. We may talk about spiritual elitism rather than class elitism, but any developmental theory implies that certain ways of living are better than others.

I don't have a great deal of trouble with elitism. The question for me is not whether or not there is an elite. There is in every society. The question is what one does with the fact of privilege.

I think it is true that I am one of the elite, as you are also. I am one of the elite in many ways, in terms of intelligence, education, personal appearance, and energy. I don't think that is a neurotic claim. I think it is a fact, a grace if you will, for which I am not responsible. To a large extent, my abilities, my gifts, are exactly that. They are gifts. One gift, for instance, is that I am much less deeply wounded than some. I have fewer abandonment fears because my parents were very loving. They were fanatical, but they were loving. I had an incredible amount of nurture, an incredible amount of richness given to me.

My question involves what people do with their gifts. I think all kinds of elites bear gifts that are needed by the body politic. These gifts are not neurotic claims. They are gifts to be reinvested.

There are various kinds of elites. There are elitists of action. I happen to be among those who are reflectional. Perhaps, I am also among the visionary elite. There are political elitists. There are financial elitists. I am not among those who are elite financially.

I don't have any trouble with these elitists, even those who are financially elite. What I do have trouble with is when a gift is distorted by becoming a neurotic claim to superiority. The Rockefellers are an example. I have a problem with the ideology that sees their wealth as proof that God has chosen the Rockefellers to be the guardians of capitalism. Their wealth is a fact, a gift to be used for the body politic. It is not a token of moral superiority.

Personal Transformation Is a Privilege

Keen: It is also true that the opportunity for personal transformation is a privilege. A lot of people do not have this
privilege. Those wandering around homeless in Cambodia,
Africa, and other places in the world, people who do not
know where their next meal is coming from, cannot be
worried too much about the condition of their souls. Practical
concerns consume their time.

I think one of the obligations that we as Americans have
comes from the fact that we are *all* elitists in a special sense.
We have enjoyed a level of material prosperity that is un-
heard of in human history and we enjoy an unparalleled level
of opportunity. Our sin is not in our opulence. Our sin lies in
the selfishness with which we have used that opulence. It is
not unlike the sin of those who are selfish with wealth, intelligence, or physical beauty. The fact is that some people get
more of the royal jelly than others. All privilege needs to be
owned, quite frankly, and used responsibly.

The Passion-Compassion Link

Keen: A second point links personal and communal transformation. The more I am in touch with myself and my own
body, the more I am in touch with other people. There is an
integral link between passion and compassion. I talked about
this in *To a Dancing God.* The more I feel my flesh, the more
horrifying it becomes to me that people should ever violate
the flesh. My response to seeing pictures of torture in Vietnam, and of homelessness, is to want to vomit, because I am
in touch with my own body and I know that what hurts me
hurts others.

To my way of thinking, there is a built-in link between real
responsiveness to my inner plurality and to the plurality that

exists outside me. The injunction in the New Testament to "Love your neighbor as yourself," is not just a commandment. It is a fact. It is a fact that I can tolerate in others only what I tolerate in myself. Only to the extent that I can say "Yes" to myself can I say "Yes" to others.

The example of therapists is important here. Most therapists are limited by their fear of insanity. They are frightened by pain. They cannot say "Yes" to insanity or "Yes" to pain. They try to put people out of their pain quickly. They try to tranquilize them. They try to get them sane again instead of being with them in the process.

In this sense, each of us is always at the center of the world. I want to own that. I want to own that the most intimate territory I have been given to enjoy and to farm is this one— my body, my life. That is the territory for which I am most responsible, and it is my link to the body politic.

But What Is the Range of Responsibility?

Fowler: What are your own theological or quasi-theological beliefs, Sam, about who is responsible? I hear you talking about a limited liability, really, as something that ought to be embraced and affirmed. What kind of a time frame are we living in with respect to responsibility?

Keen: The problem I have with the idea of responsibility is that it is both a very important idea and a very nebulous one. Sometimes I feel very responsible for myself. At other times I notice that on those days when my moods swing from high to low, from depression to elation, the tides in the ocean are also in the maximum swing from high to low. Then I say to myself, "Well, isn't that interesting! Whatever the moon is doing to the tides of the ocean, it is also in some way doing to my body." It happens every month. And always I forget. I say, "What the hell's the matter with me? What's happening? I have to find out why I'm so edgy." I look. Full moon. In ways I don't understand, the cosmos affects the chemistry of my psyche. It acts upon me. I am both a cause and an effect of action.

There is some way in which personal responsibility is too narrow a notion. The very rhythms of my body are influenced by the environment around me in very real ways. In buildings, for instance, our electrical energies are all influenced by the amount of steel used in the structure. The ion content of the air influences our bodies. We are all affected by each other all the time. We are affected by the mental sets brought by the people present. I do things very differently with a person or a group that is friendly than with one that is hostile.

The moral paradox is that I must act as if I were totally responsible but with the realization that I am not. My body type, my genetic makeup, is something that was handed to me. I'm responsible for doing what I can do with that. My society, the male capitalistic way of structuring life, is also me. I didn't choose that either in a very deep sense. It chose me. At some point in my life, which I call the Outlaw Stage, I have the option of looking at my "fate" and of undoing a lot of it.

Responsibility and Cultural-Emotional Revolution

Fowler: Let's talk about the responsibility we have in this inequality of gifts. Is that responsibility to change the unequal distribution of gifts? There is a sense in which these gifts are not just fortune's gifts, not just fate, not just God's gifts. Should we erase the blackboard and act to change this distribution?

Keen: On the way to talking about responsibility, let me begin by talking about three kinds of change, three patterns of faith. A diagram would look something like this:

Table 3.1

	AGE 0		AGE 40		AGE 80
Pattern:	Child	Rebel	Adult	Outlaw	Lover/Fool
I. Unborn					
II. "Once-born"					
III. "Multi-born"					

The first pattern is that of the "Unborn" person. This kind of person starts at age one and goes to age eighty without moving up or down on the emotional scale. He or she gets no farther than the Adult stage, so that in some sense there is no real progression in life. There is certainly no revolution in the psychological sense.

We all know a lot of people like this. At age forty they are exactly what they were at age fourteen. They follow the path like a man I was talking to the other day who in his late forties still looked like a boy. He said that he had come to the workshop I was offering to "grow up." When the meeting was over, he said that the evening was very significant because he had started getting angry at his father.

He began to tell me about his father. He had been a Buick salesman and then the manager of a Buick agency, then an insurance agent and then a broker. "Wait a minute?" I asked him, "Didn't you tell me that *you* had been a Buick salesman and then the manager of a Buick agency. Didn't you tell me that you also went on to become an insurance salesman and then a broker?"

He said, "Yes."

This man is an example of one who was unborn. Until he was forty-eight he had never experienced his own life in a psychological sense. He had only been possessed.

The second pattern is that of the "Once-born." The once-born make a gentle rise throughout their lives. This terminology comes from William James,[3] and he refers to nurture when he talks about the once-born. These people don't have revolutions either. They grow and they continue.

The third pattern is that of the "Multi-born." The multi-born personality lives in up and down movement. There are crisis points. Each transition is marked by a life crisis until at midlife there is a radical rebirth. As Dante said, in the middle of life's journey he found himself in a dark wood. Coming out of this forest is the second birth.

I think that we can look at social growth as well as personal psychological growth in terms of these patterns. What we have in American society is a preference for the once-born. We don't like radical transitions. We try to steer clear of revolutions; we prefer evolution. I feel that we have reached the point where we *must* look at the multi-born experience. At America's bicentennial, she is dead. Vietnam was America's midlife crisis. Capitalism as a total way of organizing the world has been shown to be corrupt. The unequal distribution of wealth, our carelessness of the environment, and our insane military responses to minor crises have made this clear.

One way to redistribute the unequal gifts and to meet the challenges of limited resources is exemplified by China. Without glorifying the Chinese experiment, and I am sure there is much tyranny in it, I see in their system some ways that are promising in terms of the sharing of gifts. Intellectuals there learn to labor and laborers learn to be more intellectual about their labor. We need to stop the incredible specialization that we have at the emotional and cultural level. We need a revolution at this level, and I look forward to it.

Individuals and Communities

Fowler: How do we who deal in developmental structures deal with that? How do we make our individuation not individualistic? The approach that you just described puts great premium on making the Outlaw just another version of the "rugged individual," which in a sense is a very American image.

Keen: In the Outlaw and the Lover stages of development there is a softening of the personality. It becomes more and more inclusive. It incorporates more of the feminine virtues. These are not capitalist virtues.

Fowler: Once we have a community and a covenant, I am concerned about the social construction and reconstruction of reality. What we have said so far is that we have to accept the social construction of reality that puts us in armor up to the point that we either come to our senses or shake out of the armor and become naked and vulnerable. We also become audacious and like Prometheus steal the fire and try to give it to mankind for its benefit. What community can we tie into? What can we create?

Keen: I am like everybody else. I don't have many answers to the problem of community. The lack of an answer is a symptom of where we are. Community is something we all long for. We all realize how necessary it is to learn how to recreate it. The fact is that we do not yet know where the community lies in the future. None of the theories really help. The old theory that says a covenant came first doesn't help because it doesn't take into consideration the discontinuity we have to overcome before we are able to commit ourselves to a covenant and a community.

In some sense, my schema has been a lifeboat for me. When I reached the point where the traditional covenants—church, university—were killing me, I had to make the choice between discontinuity and death. I knew at the time I broke continuity that there was something terribly tragic about it. I knew my decision involved cruelties and hurting people. But, somehow, I knew that in order to live I had to make those decisions.

After making the decision for discontinuity and trying to live for a long time without covenants and without commitments, I discovered that I couldn't live like that either. When life becomes a series of one-night stands, it is not very pleasurable. It is not rich for you or anyone else. There is a kind of betrayal in living in and for the moment.

Lack of commitment is as much a betrayal as covenants without girth and flexibility are. Emotional, cultural, geographical, and political one-night stands are a form of betrayal. As the French say, "The more things change the more they stay the same." I know a lot of people who practice the "California Ethic" and live a life of one-night stands, but in their variety they have no variety. All they do is to go to first base a hundred times—sexually, emotionally, or otherwise.

Symbol-Making and Symbol-Makers

Fowler: You vigorously disagreed with me during my initial presentation on the question of symbols, and we promised to come back to that. It seems to me that communities in some ways form around symbols. They also produce and refill symbols as they have shared experiences. Where do we disagree?

Keen: There is a deep-seated tradition that says we move away from symbols as we develop. There is an increasing falling away from symbols and the relationship with symbols. The Zen tradition is an example. The young man sees the tree as a tree and the mountain as a mountain. He ponders this and then no longer sees them as such. He becomes confused. As an old man, he again sees them simply as a tree and a mountain.

Ludwig Wittgenstein also talked about this.[4] He wondered why so many people who had been to the other side had nothing to tell when they came back. The reason is that there is nothing to tell. Nothing has been changed. It's just that a tree is a tree and a chair is a chair. It's just that I'm not arguing with myself about that any longer. It's not that the picture on the television is any different; it's just that the static is gone. There is a grace in moving through this world and an acceptance of what it is. Tillich referred to this state as "self-transcending realism."[5]

I, in fact, depend less and less on symbols. I have less and less patience with any kind of high symbolism. To me, the Lord's Supper as practiced in most churches is a sad kind of ritualistic excuse for not eating with people. The more I experience the substance of things, the less I need the forms. But that may be temperamental. It might be due to something deep in my iconoclastic nature or to the Quaker side of me.

Fowler: John Calvin's Geneva was pretty sparse of symbols.

Keen: Yes, but it was also sparse of joy. There was little real celebration. They did not want emotional excess. I do. I want emotional excess. I want the epiphanies.

Fowler: Yet, you are a very prolific maker of symbols. . . .

Keen: You noticed, didn't you. That brings us to a very important point, and you are exactly right. I am a maker of symbols. I have found out that the more I insist on being Sam Keen and experiencing "his journey," the more I find out that it is everybody else's journey. My life is filled with all kinds of mythical resonances. Prometheus did it before I did. Adam did it before I did. Ulysses was on the same journey. I find myself inhabited by a community of experiences that enriches me. The myths resonate in me and vice versa. But it doesn't help me much if I try to look at the map before I take the trip.

Fowler: That's what I meant when I said "refilling" symbols. I meant the discovery that a symbol epitomizes something that we are experiencing with an economy and a force and under a universality that our other modes of discourse cannot capture.

I think that faith as trust involves us not only in interpersonal trust in each other, but, as I said in my initial presentation, I also follow Josiah Royce in his claim that we are loyal to each other, not just because of each other, but because we have shared loyalties. There are causes to which we are loyal that both reinforce and are the context for our interpersonal loyalties. It is Durkheim's idea of the collective representations, the efforts to symbolize the excellence we are aspiring to or the excellence we have been apprehended by. I think the maintenance of community requires these symbols.

Keen: It seems to me that we need to ask people like you and me, who are "intellectuals" and write books, a question about lies. In a real sense, our writings are lies, but very good lies. We write about things we do not yet know. I think of it this way: I am always at least ten years ahead of myself in my writing. One of the reasons I wrote about, and was so interested in, the Dionysian way was because I was so obviously Apollonian. I have a head like a rock. In the same way, my talk about paranoia is something I am working through. My face has far more paranoid lines than yours does. Your lines are astonishment lines. The ones on my face are paranoid lines.

The same thing is true when I say, "To hell with the Christian church." I haven't been in one in a long time and they bore me to tears. It is because that stuff is so deep in me that I don't want the symbols anymore. I cannot stand going to a service on Sunday morning. It is one of the deadliest things in my life when I have to do it. This is partly because I got the message so well that I don't need the symbols. They get in my way. I don't want them.

I was so well-trained as a Scotch Presbyterian that the message of life's being a journey and God's having a plan now leads me to say, "To hell with Calvin," and mean it at this point in my life. I think it is a question of where you come from. The Christian community is not very important to me anymore because it is in my bones. I don't have to talk Christian talk all the time.

Fowler: What new symbols have you come up with to replace the symbols of the Christian community?

Keen: As you have noticed, a lot of my symbols are radically demythologized Christian symbols. My talk about "novelty" is an example. My language is covertly Christian, you might say, but it is calculated to get across to people who don't come in with a Bible in hand.

In terms of an overarching symbol for my life? Last year I finished *Beginnings Without End.* In that book I trace the last four years of my life of radical discontinuities and the dawning realization that I can begin again. For me, right now, my overarching myth is that life is a process which is full of beginnings that have no end. It is very Christian, but it is Christian in a way that church institutions have denied in practice. The institutions have kept us from beginning again.

When I talk about "brokenness," I am talking about the Christian doctrine of sin. The institutional church has blocked this, too, by its lack of faith. They won't let you be a "sinner." You cannot laugh, have an erection, or be angry in church. Seeing sin as brokenness makes clear that the church is still one of the major places where the split between the body and the mind is kept alive. It is the place where sexuality is most denigrated. The theology of the church lifts up wholeness and says that the spirit has come into matter. But it is antisensual in practice. It talks theoretically about psychosomatic joining, and yet it communicates brokenness.

In a sense, the problem of the church is a problem of our culture. This brokenness is nowhere more evident or better symbolized than in medical centers around the world. Huge hospitals are built to care for the body, but no one asks about what disease means. You could take the heart out and replace it with a machine without asking why the heart broke in the first place. I think that we need specialists in wholeness more than we need surgeons or psychiatrists.

My answers to the question of symbol-making are personal. I am trying to be very responsible to my own culture and my own story. My answers are practical. They are answers that work for me.

Fowler: Sam, I know you would not want to be forced into the posture of giving answers for other people. I know you don't claim that, yet there is a strong covert invitation. But let's look at the making of a religion of the body politic and its breakup.

Social and Personal Disintegration

Fowler: Where is the civil religion taking us? What is your critique of that? How can we make sense out of the enormous disintegration or, perhaps, transition taking place in our society? As a theologian, as a maker and critic of myths, as a commentator on demythologization—where do you think truth lies in all this breakup? How can we live in this broken-ness in ways besides making of ourselves a special project and concentrating on our own wholeness and on our own journey?

Keen: I see the political crisis America has gone through as very similar to the journey I have taken personally. We are in the middle of a depression. As a nation, we are depressed, and that depression has very little to do with economics. We have an energy crisis as a nation. It is similar to what happens in a neurotic person. The depression comes from the fact that the major part of our energies is invested in defense mech-anisms. Probably half the literal substance of the country has been squandered on its paranoid delusions of keeping the world safe from something called communism. The whole energy thing, the crisis in the economy, is merely a reflection of a deeper spiritual crisis.

The spiritual crisis of this nation is the loss of a vision of who and what we are. It is in this sense, I think, that people without a vision die. If America, as a nation, does not create a vision of what it is about, then, increasingly it will go the secular route to its decline. It will have excluded the possibility of its rebirth.

Theological Education:
Guiding Religious Experience
Gossip and Hearsay Evidence

Keen: I was on the Association of Theological Schools' Committee for Change of Theological Education in the 1970s. At the time I was serving on that Committee, I put forth a thesis, timidly, that I wish now I had had the sense to be obnoxious about. I wasn't. I was nice and I was polite. They laughed and said, "Oh, that's very clever." After the report was published, I should have written a comment stating that it was a lie and nothing more than another compromise with the heart of the matter.

What I suggested was that seminary education should take its model from the shaman rather than from the priest. The shaman is a kind of religious person who has the courage to go into the depths. The shaman knows the underworld and the overworld. He talks out of his own experience rather than gossiping about other people's experience. Seminary education consists largely of gossiping about religious experience, and it is afraid of religious ecstasy or any other excess.

The priestly tradition in seminary education has interlocked with other forces to leave us with a situation in which most people who go into the ministry are passive, dependent males who have incredible problems with females. They are coming into mother church. Given these views, it is not surprising that I have been invited to speak at only one seminary in the past seven years.

I personally believe deeply in theological training, but I believe it is being done totally wrong. The question being asked now is: "How can the church survive?" The question should be: "How can we become initiated into the depths of human experience?"

Theological education needs to address itself to divine madness. If it does, its authority will return and the minister as shaman will have an important place in society. I recommend Joseph Campbell's *The Hero with a Thousand Faces*[6] as a textbook for the religious journey.

Fowler: I suppose I am still at the point of putting it the way Sam Keen did in his report and maybe not even that strongly. Among other things, I began teaching in a theological school with a commitment to helping students come to grips with the history they have lived through by drawing upon the experiences they have had. The thing that I hear Sam saying, though, is a forceful way of stating something that I tried to approach earlier when I talked about the taboos which I take to be the boundaries of our "armor" in Sam's metaphor.

The taboos I have spoken about here and elsewhere during the last few years are the ones that really give us fundamental anxiety about stepping beyond certain boundaries. The clergy person has to be one who has plumbed the depths of spiritual insight as well as the hells that go with that. I have not said it with the radicality that Sam Keen has said it. I have not lived it with the radicality that he has lived it. It costs. The price tags emotionally and socially for the kind of journey that goes into the depths and gets inside of things are very high.

I think that theology right now is in a terrible academic captivity. I think there is an incestuous quality that is present in that captivity which comes from theologians' writing for other theologians. The work I am trying to do now is in part a corrective to that. I am trying to get out into the context of where people are forming and reforming their lives. The thing that devils me in the process, however, is how we ourselves as teachers break through the crust of culture. How also do we enable our students to break through that crust? That crust is sustaining, but it is also constricting. How can theological education be more comfortable with wildness and chaos? How can it be more at home with the unmanageability of things?

It seems to me that there is a model for this. Jesus is such a model for that kind of life. I think, politically speaking, it does mean some sort of radical identification with those to whom Jesus came and with the oppressed and the exploited of any time, including our own. It is there, I would say, that our compassion ought to be tested. I enjoy this kind of gathering very much, but that is where we probably should go to do theology.

It is my feeling that Sam speaks a true word about the university, the church, and the theological seminary, but there is still something that bothers me in what he is saying. This prevents me from being a complete "me-too-er." To only say this much is to be incomplete.

I am married. I am monogamously married and I have been married for thirteen years. I married as a kid, at twenty-one, and my wife and I during the thirteen years since then have with fair, honest struggle together plumbed a number of depths of human despair and human ecstasy. What I want to state is that there is also a way for the once-born to search these depths and to be authentic in that search. I am trying to say that this kind of life too is a destiny, a personal myth, a more once-born Promethianism, but just as valid.

It is also my feeling that there is a kind of theological education for the once-born. Everyone need not be required to sell all that he has and to give it to the poor or to plunge through all the old taboos. There is a way to sponsor a kind of authenticity of experiencing and of drawing upon experience in theological education for the once-born, too. It has to do with being honest and engaging in mutual listening.

It has been my experience that students are most liberated when I am able to say to them, "I am extraordinarily perplexed over this problem, too. Let me share with you the way it looks perplexing to me." I like to invite the student into the problem. I used to worry about teaching stuff that was ahead of where I knew I was going. I discovered, though, that the lectures I thought were best, the most logically finished and closed, gave no way to the student to get involved in them. The ones with interstices drew them in, and they became colleagues with me in a wrestling with the mysteries. They drew on their experience and perceptions, as I did on mine. The apron strings from the authorities were cut. The gossiping stopped.

Clergy persons, theological professors, and professors generally need to make themselves a good bit more vulnerable by opening up questions they have and by including the students in them. But in addition to opening up, there is the question of hearing. Hearing on both sides is incredibly important.

I have already described the experiences we have had with the faith interviews. We have all had to work to be listeners and to hear. We all tend to be talkers. Hearing is an acutely active, engaging enterprise. My work at Interpreter's House was to listen. Once, when conducting an interview for a prospective "listener," I blew up when he said to me, "I don't

know if I could take this job, because it is such a passive job."
I had been learning over and over during my time there how
exacting and active a work it is to hear out people and to do
that hermeneutical act of enabling them to say to you what
they otherwise could not, but needed to, say.

Listening is crucial not only to the more "educational" task
of formal teaching and learning but to the preaching act as
well. Sermons need to be the product of listening and hearing.
When the speaking begins, it should be a response to what
one has heard during one's active listening.

Keen: I agree, and I realize that what I have said could
easily be misinterpreted. My particular way has been more
the twice-born than the once-born journey. I am also aware,
however, that my journey has been more disruptive to myself
and others than I wished. There are tragic discontinuities in
my life, the major one being that I do not live with my
children. I bear guilt about that, and sorrow, but I am not
ashamed.

In a society that was functioning right, I think, there would
be fewer patterns of the twice-born variety and there would
be more once-born journeys. I fault education for this. Education for many of us has meant that we either had to live with
the discontinuities or die, and we had no idea that there was
another way besides the approved once-born way. Education
did not teach us techniques for transcending and descending,
techniques many need for survival.

My essay "Education for Serendipity," which is published
in *To a Dancing God,* was a start at saying what education
would look like in a healthy society. More once-born
journeys would be possible there, and twice-born people
would have better techniques to make their way in the world,
too.

I know a bit more now about education than I did when I wrote that, and I am more than ever convinced that the main thing that needs to be introduced is a more primitive approach. We need more techniques that touch the affective domain.

We need, for example, to teach people to stay in touch with their dreams. Dreams are the opening edge of our craziness. If you stay in touch with your dreams, you will probably not have to make a crazy journey. You will be able to make a once-born journey.

Second, if we teach people to maintain touch with their own bodies, that will also help. Teaching direct experiential disciplines, like meditation and sensory awareness, or unconscious awareness and the reading of unconscious symbolism, will help. We know how to do this now, but it is being done largely under the guise of therapy rather than as education. This awareness is crucial to enable people to move through life without having to tear up everything around them to make their journey. They should have more gentle techniques at hand. The tragedy of our society is that so few of us (especially the elite who got there because their heads were hard as rocks) can learn to soften our heads without some other part of the body running away for awhile.

Fowler: Sometimes these techniques lie in unexpected places or in places that are overlooked because of misunderstanding or excessive familiarity. I last discovered this (and one discovers it over and over) when I began working on the faith development project. I realized that I was getting awfully Apollonian and awfully dry. "Dry" is almost an understatement. I was virtually shipwrecked in terms of being cast upon the sand away from the water.

In my class that year there was a group of Jesuits. They

kept saying in subtle ways that Ignatian spirituality was becoming very important to the Jesuits again. It might be important for me too. My image of Saint Ignatius was not an inviting one, but the Jesuits kept at it in a persistent, gentle, brotherly way. Finally, one of them gave me a copy of *The Spiritual Exercises*,[7] written by Saint Ignatius. It is not a very edifying book to read, at least not prior to any experience in using it.

I went to a Jesuit Spiritual Director in Cambridge and said, "Look, I need some help. My own prayer life and my living with the Scriptures is all dried up. I'm in trouble."

He said, "I don't know if I can help you or not," but he took me on in an extended retreat. With great gentleness and in a unique relationship—not as a therapist or pastor in the sense of having answers, but more like a coach—he introduced me to the "new" method that he taught.

"I want you to take this story of the feeding of the 5,000, and I want you to meditate on it for three days. Just spend an hour a day. I want you to start off just mastering the thing. Use your cognitive abilities to get every detail of the story. Get everything down. Repeat it so that the narrative gets into you.

"The next day I want you to try to let loose of what you did the day before. Now I want you to read yourself into the story. I want you to sensually participate in it. I want you to smell the smells of that crowd. I want you to hear the sounds of their voices. I want you to feel them jostling up against you. I want you to see them and to see Jesus. Above all, I want you to taste that food. Above all, I want you to taste it."

Some extraordinary things began to happen as I followed his directions. On the third day my task was to let my mind play. I was to let it be open to my own hungers. I was to ask myself what I was hungry for. Where did I need to be fed?

Who feeds me? What food is there that I cannot get along without?

I discovered a porousness between my conscious and my unconscious mind. Images began to rise and meet images from the story. It was almost as if that part of me which is usually in control was in neutral. A new kind of transaction between myself and the text began to occur. I began to see how that tradition could be an instrument of the spirit in a way and degree that were different from anything I had known before.

I got in touch with my needs, with my hungers. I found a vulnerability. And I found a mediator. All this was in a way that I had not found from using my cognitive approach. I think that the sort of method found in the *Spiritual Exercises* is very promising for groups and for individuals. It is a native, Christian, and Western method of doing some of the things that we are learning about from other sources. Ignatius was very much like Carl Jung in his understanding of the way the unconscious produces symbols that can depict our situation, our needs, our directional tendency.

Keen: There are hundreds of such things that would become available to us if only we began to integrate them. The whole human potential movement has been nothing more than a lightly secularized exploration of religious disciplines. There has been work in the areas of dreaming, of sensory awareness, of drugs (which have always been in the religious tradition), meditation, the realm of the imagination—all those things. We are learning a lot about such things and there is no mystery to the techniques.

Not only is a lot known about such techniques, but there is also a great hunger for what they can give. The fact that these techniques can be found outside of organized religion also has been helpful for people who are truly searching. There is more permission to undertake a radical search outside religious institutions, more permission to use these techniques that were traditionally used by religions.

The kind of education we need is no mystery. It used to be stated that we could teach people how to read Kant but that we could not educate them to get in touch with their feelings. That is not true now and probably never was. There are appropriate means for affective education. There are appropriate means for initiating the young into the depths and the heights of human experience. As we have both said, a desperate need of our time is to use such means to continue the human journey toward deepening trust.

References:* Dialogue

1. William F. Lynch, *Images of Hope* (Baltimore: Helicon Press, 1965).

2. Erik H. Erikson, *Toys and Reasons* (New York: W. W. Norton, 1977).

3. William James, *The Varieties of Religious Experience* (New York: Mentor Books, 1958). First published in 1902.

4. Ludwig Wittgenstein held that deep tautologies show certain general features of the world such as its "logical properties" or the "scaffolding of the world." There is something beneath them which is trying to get out to find a different form of expression. In the *Tractatus Logico-Philosophicus*, trans. D. F. Pears and B. F. McGuinness (London: Routledge & Kegan Paul; New York: The Humanities Press, 1961), he said: "For what the solipsist *means* is quite correct; only it cannot be *said*, but makes itself manifest." See 5.62(2). Again: "There are, indeed, things that cannot be put into words. They *make themselves manifest*. They are what is mystical."

5. Paul Tillich, *The Protestant Era* (Chicago: University of Chicago Press, 1948), pp. 66-68. On p. 67, he writes: "Self-transcending realism combines two elements, the emphasis on the real and the transcending power of faith. There seems to be no wider gap than that between a realistic and belief-ful attitude. Faith transcends every conceivable reality; realism questions every transcending of the real, calling it utopian or romantic. Such a tension is hard to stand, and it is not surprising that the human mind always tries to evade it." A later, more systematic treatment of self-transcendence can be found in *Systematic Theology*, Vol. 3 (Chicago: University of Chicago Press, 1963), pp. 86-98. It is in the context of life as the actualization of potential through the three functions of self-integration, self-creativity, and self-transcendence.

6. Joseph Campbell, *The Hero with a Thousand Faces* (Princeton, N.J.: Princeton University Press, 1968).

7. Ignatius de Loyola, *The Spiritual Exercises of St. Ignatius*, trans. Anthony Mottola (New York: Doubleday).

*Ed.

Continuing the Conversation: A Non-Concluding Postscript

The purpose of adding a new chapter to the second edition of *Life Maps* is to stress one word in the book's subtitle. This word and the spirit it intended to convey about the book got lost in the background of other concerns for many readers as the first edition went through several printings. What is the word? It is "Conversations."

Many reviewers and other readers of *Life Maps* tended to focus on either Fowler or Keen. Few noticed the delightful interplay between them and between the models of faith development which they proposed. It is to that interplay the reader's attention is directed now by this new chapter.

The interplay between the views and persons of Fowler and Keen connects in many different ways and at many different levels. One might say, for example, that the differences between them are so great that they cannot be rationally compared. Preference would have to be judged on the basis of taste as if one were comparing two kinds of fruit and preferred apples over oranges or vice-versa.

Another way to look at the interplay between Fowler

and Keen is to say that they are playing the same game, but that they are on two different sides. When they entered into the game they entered into a relationship which required one of them to win and one of them to lose. It was not the intention of anyone to put them into such an adversary relationship but the academic debate setting imposed it on them.

The debate setting was acknowledged by the use of such terms as "loving combat" and "assaults." Sometimes such an adversary relationship can help clarify problems and find their best solution. Other times the observers merely take up sides with the combatants and cheer for their favorites. Both responses have resulted from reading this book, as they did in the original 1975 conference, but there is more to *Life Maps* than that.

A third way to look at the interplay between Fowler and Keen is to think of it as a search for points of view by which to observe a single phenomenon. Words such as "perspectives" and "views" acknowledged this interpretation. It was as if Fowler and Keen were in basic agreement about the value and existence of the faith phenomenon and were looking at it from two standpoints. The judgment in this case is not an "either/or" type. It is more "both/and" in character. It assumes one can know more about faith by using both standpoints than could be known by using either point of view alone.

There is a fourth way that *Life Maps* might be read. One might consider the two faith development models to be so closely related as to be complementary models. The weakness of one model might fit with the strength of the other one. This is to suggest more than that the models are two good points of view. It adds to this conclusion the suggestion that the two views are interlocking.

One might also read the book in a fifth way. It might be read from a systems point of view. The two models might be considered as two subsystems in a larger whole. The larger system might be an experiential theology which cannot be understood apart from the core theological virtues of faith, hope, and love, as St. Paul suggested in his First Letter to the Church at Corinth.

A sixth way to read the interaction between Fowler and Keen is to experience it as a recapitulation of the creative process at work. The new ideas generated and challenged feed back into the reader's own engendering of new discoveries about his or her own faith patterns. Fowler and Keen might even represent different parts of the process by their contrasts. Reading Fowler might be more like the working out of one's intuitions into concepts and testing them. Keen's way of working may be more attuned to the testing out of one's first intuitions and scanning for a resolution. A reader's preference might say more about his or her own tendency toward an aspect of the whole creative process at work than a critical and objective evaluation of the models presented.

One might also enjoy the interplay between Fowler and Keen in a seventh way. One might delight not only in the horizontal interaction but also the vertical interaction among the many levels of interpretation.

An eighth way one might look at this book is as if it were a kind of allegory. Perhaps, *Life Maps* is about two aspects of the dynamic impulse of life. The figures of Fowler and Keen stand for such forces at work creating new life. To read *Life Maps* is to experience the Creator creating in these creatures the ability to "create" creating in each other.

All of this is a bit farfetched. As *Life Maps* is thought about, re-read, and discussed, such talk of levels should probably be forgotten. The book is complicated enough without suggesting that there might be something in the background interacting with the perceived main line of the text. The book is probably too insubstantial to warrant such speculations, and, besides, it is bad form for the book's editor to make such observations. We should turn, therefore, at once to the rather straightforward chapter now before you. It has four sections and all have to do with map-making.

The first section deals with the linguistic tools needed for making faith maps. The tools discussed are symbols, metaphors, models, and paradigms. The second section discusses cartographers, because the making of maps cannot be untangled from the mapmakers. Thirdly, the chapter looks at the maps themselves and the image of "development" by which change, permanence and faith are related to each other. Finally, the fourth section deals with mapping maps. It is an effort to provide the reader with the perspective by which to compare one's own faith development with the models of Fowler and Keen.

This new chapter for the second edition of *Life Maps* is an invitation to the reader to playfully enter into the Fowler and Keen conversation. It is an invitation to question their tools, their trustworthiness as cartographers, the kinds of maps drawn, and to ponder one's own assumptions about what a life map ought to be. We turn first to the questioning of what the best tools are to make such maps.

Tools to Make Maps

This first section to our "Non-Concluding Postscript" is about map-making tools. It will use the metaphor of making geographical maps to enrich the discussion of what tools are needed to fashion models of faith development. The metaphor of the geographical map will be used throughout this chapter to discuss life maps with an emphasis on the journey of faith.

The discussion of tools will turn first to how map-making tools are used in the discovery of new lands and states of knowing. Secondly, we will outline the kinds of tools for geographical and faith maps. Finally, we will compare two kinds of maps, the theological and the scientific. This will prepare us for the section that will follow which will be about the map-makers themselves and their methods.

The discovery of new lands and states of knowing seems to have three major steps. There is first the formation of the focus on the goal of the voyage. Columbus wanted to go to India. This begins a process of organizing and interpreting "facts" in relationship to that goal. Prediction plays back and forth with the descriptions of those who have already made the voyage and returned with news of the dangers and best routes.

A second step is to compile all that is known and guessed about. The means for this piling up of fact and interpretation is thinking. Images and words generated from the facts and guesses play back and forth with the possible coherence in a map. The map is made and the voyage is begun.

The third step is the checking of the predicted pattern in reality with the actual voyage. The interplay of map and trip results in new descriptions and more detailed maps for future voyages.

The patterns in awareness, the semantic form, and the bearing on reality of the synthesis — all are important. We will focus here on the semantic form or second step and take a closer look at these semantic tools we have at hand by which maps of faith can be fashioned. We will look now at symbols, metaphors, models, and paradigms.

A symbol is something that stands for something else. This "standing-for-something-else" includes many kinds of references. A map for example stands for the actual world. The word, "map," stands for the cartographer's concept of the world.

Symbols may narrowly or broadly define the relationship between them and the world. The term, "H_2O," in the language of chemistry neatly reproduces the molecular structure it points to. In the language of Christianity, however, the term, "water," evokes many levels of meaning and a whole network of associations from the waters of destruction in the flood to the waters of purification and regeneration in the rite of baptism. Sometimes this narrow and broad use of symbols is distinguished by calling the narrow indicator a "sign" and the broad indicator a "symbol."

A second tool the cartographer uses is the metaphor. It does not merely name something else like a sign or symbol does. It creates its meaning by connecting a likeness and unlikeness in the two entities related. To say that "the tiger is a lion," however, is very different from saying that "the man is a lion." A distance is also required between the two connected entities for a metaphor to do its work well.

The two related entities in a metaphor sometimes stir deep emotions. Such powerful metaphors are not improved by translating them into nonmetaphoric form. The tension between what is said and what is not said is lost and the emotional depth connecting the two frames of reference can be extinguished.

This is not to say that a translation of a metaphoric statement is not useful. It can be very useful, because a metaphor can also be turned into an analogy and extended into a model.

An analogy makes an explicit comparison between something that is known and something that is unknown, so the unknown term can be better understood. Metaphors involve what is not said as much as what is said, but analogies focus on saying as much as possible about the unknown. When the unknown is understood the analogy is no longer needed. A metaphor can also cease to function as such, but it is not because the unknown aspect of life it points to is understood completely. The metaphor becomes dormant when its use becomes a habit. An example is a table "leg" or a chair "arm." These metaphors are disfunctional as metaphors but remain useful as signs.

A third kind of mapping tool is the model. It has some characteristics of a metaphor but is more like an analogy extended to become more systematic and complex. A model communicates a whole system rather than a few salient points like an analogy does or the juxtapositions of likes and unlikes which the metaphor conveys. The sentence, "A person is like a machine," can be extended, for example, to show human functions in detail.

Ian Barbour suggested that there are four basic kinds of models:[1]

1. Scale models reproduce all the features of the reality being modeled. A small working model of an actual locomotive or sailing ship are examples. When the model needed cannot be reproduced by an exact replica that is smaller or larger, then, another kind of model is needed.
2. Logical models are constructed from axioms and theorems. They work in the realm of ideas by means of a formal deductive system. They are the opposite of scale models, because there is no immediate connection to a specific physical system.
3. Mathematical models stand between the extremes of the experimental and logical models. They are symbolic representations of quantitative variables in physical or social systems. They resemble the primary system only in formal structure.
4. Theoretical models are imaginative mental constructions

which account for observed phenomena. The imagined systems propose analogies between the known and the unknown.

The primary focus here is on theoretical models. The "billiard-ball" model of gas is a good example. It was used by Barbour. Common air is the gas we will think about.

Let us suppose that we can compress air by a piston in a container like a bicycle pump. When the gas is compressed the pressure increases inside the tube. We can feel this as the pump handle goes down and we know the air will go into the flat tire because of this increased pressure. Why? We need a model for gas to be able to explain what we have observed about the relationship between the compression of air and the pressure in the enclosed container.

A successful model was proposed by Robert Boyle (1627–1691), an English physicist and chemist. He said that gas is composed of very tiny elastic spheres. We can't see them, but let us suppose that this is the case. Let us suppose further that they have a mechanical kind of behavior, like colliding billiard balls.

It was such thinking, guided by the model proposed, that resulted in Boyle's Law. This law says that if the volume of gas is reduced by half, then, the pressure of the gas in the closed container is doubled. When this law is tested against our experience in the world it turns out to be a good description which reproduces what actually happens.

A good model needs to be intelligible as a unity so it can be grasped as a whole. It also needs to be detailed enough to suggest how theories can be extended from it.

The fourth and final cartographer's tool we will discuss is the paradigm. It is often used without realizing it. When we said "mechanical kind of behavior" above to conceptualize the colliding billiard balls in the model for gas, we inferred a paradigm. It was a view of the world as if it worked like a machine. We still use this paradigm today although it was most powerful when thinking was filled with images of levers, pulleys, cogs, waterwheels, and steam engines. Newton's sweeping mechanical view of physics which dominated the imagination of science for two centuries.

Large interpretative frameworks called paradigms shape our observations, the questions we ask, the models we use, and the criteria established for verification and falsification.[2] They provide the ultimate limits within which a particular language domain such as physics can conceive of its models, invent with its metaphors, and define its symbols.

It is like sailing out into the unknown in our models as if they were ships. We live in them. The chart of the whole voyage for this ship, however, is the paradigm. Both Fowler and Keen have presented models for faith development in which a faith journey might be taken. One wonders what the larger paradigm or map is for each of their models that shapes its meaning. We also need to know what each cartographer thinks about the status of the relationship between the model and the reality modeled.

To begin this discussion about the status of models we need to play with the image of the map a bit more. Much of the power of maps comes from their ability to bring things into relationship with other things that are difficult to see together. A story from Aelian's *Various Histories*[3] is a classic example. Socrates wearied of Alcibiades' constant boasting about his wealth and land holdings. Socrates took him to a place in Athens, the story goes, where a map of the known world had been placed. He asked Alcibiades to point out Attica, the state surrounding Athens, and he did.

Socrates than asked him to point out his private lands. "But they are not there," Alcibiades exclaimed. Socrates replied, "How can you boast so much about something that is not even shown as part of the earth!"

Maps can carry a kind of authority by their physical presence. Even mistakes made by cartographers become official. We who are called "Americans" rather than "Columbians" are heirs of such a mistake.

David Greenhood called the authority maps imposed "cartophobia."[4] Sometimes people are unwilling to put their imaginations to work when confronted by a map. Confusion from not knowing how to read maps combines with the map's implicit argument that the world is the way the map pictures it. It almost requires the presence of a new map or paradigm to refute an old one.

Cartophobia prevents people from playing with maps and using them *as if they were real* instead of reality itself. This happens despite knowing that the blue river on the map is not wet and the yellow area marked as desert is not made of sand. Even though we know that the peeling from an orange cannot be spread out flat on the table without splitting to pieces, we still think that the round world's map spread out flat the way the real earth is.

Maps of the earth can teach us much about life maps. The earliest priorities of chartscribners were starkly realistic. Little time was spent pondering the theory of maps. Early hydrographers, for example, were interested in all aspects of the sea, but it was direction that mattered most. They did not even care as much about distance or depth. Many mistakes could be overcome on the way but without direction the journey would not reach its intended end. This is why in the third section of this chapter we will discuss the "development" image and its implicit argument about faith development's direction.

Direction, however, is not as easy to picture as it might sound. The map drawn by the monk, Matthew Paris, which is now in the British Museum is an example. It will be compared to a map drawn by a professional, Abraham Cresques, the official map and compass maker to Peter III of Aragon.[5]

The monk's map shows a series of seven coastal towns from Haifa in Palestine to Damietta in the eastern corner of the Egyptian delta. The middle city in this series of seven is Jaffa and a road leads straight from there to the holy city of Jerusalem. The sequence of the cities was important for the medieval sea traveler since it inferred direction. The straight presentation of the coast, however, put the Nile River parallel to the Jerusalem road which set Cairo straight east of Jerusalem! This would have been troublesome for a land traveler.

The World Atlas of Abraham Cresques was prepared in 1375 as a gift to the King of France. It includes a section of coast in India where the Kingdom of Delhi was in the northwestern quarter of the country. This was known to Cresques by hearsay. The map's most prominent features at first sight are medieval touches — drawings of strange kings and fantastic beasts. The most important part, however, is the constant scale, the web of compass bearings, the correct orientation of the string of coastal towns, and the fact that these towns are represented by standard symbols for towns rather than by individual pictures, as in the monk's map.

The traditions of map-makers are important. The son of Abraham Cresques went to Portugal in 1427 where a project was being discussed for sailing around Africa to reach India. He brought with him the Catalan system for drawing charts which he learned from his father. We shall have more to say about map-makers, their traditions, and their methods in the next section of this chapter.

The outside frames for early maps are especially interesting as are the outside frames of any paradigms. Sometimes direction carried the traveler to the edge and into the mists and mythical creatures drawn at the map's borders. Sometimes whole continents were left out, as Columbus discovered when he found "Indians" in America. He had ventured beyond the edge to disprove that there was no edge from which a ship might fall.

The connection between a map and reality is an interesting one, whether one is making a geographical or a spiritual journey. The status one gives models has been studied by Ian Barbour[6] and he has identified four ways that this relationship has been conceived.

Two of the views of a model's status are not used much today. They stand at the overrealistic end of the spectrum. One view is called "naive realism" which assumes that what a model names is real. A second view assumes that the model is a summary of the data. This view is called "positivism."

A third view is more in use today. It is the instrumentalist view. This standpoint assumes that models guide inquiry and help express it. They are useful fictions. Once the psychological function is satisfied and a mathematical statement has been generated about the identified reality the model can be discarded.

The fourth view is the one to which Barbour subscribes. It is the position of "critical realism." It stands between the positions of the useful fiction and naive realism. This view holds that models are human constructions that represent the world. Neither literalism nor instrumentalism can be subscribed to because the structure of the world would be inaccessible without models. They should, therefore, be seriously but not literally regarded.

Sallie McFague[7] reduced the four Barbour categories to the two most widely used today. She called them the "high" and "low" views of models. The low view recognizes the use of human imagination to discover models, so it is neither a kind of naive realism nor positivism. It is a low view of a model's usefulness once the isomorphism between the statement about the world and the world's structure itself is translated into other, usually mathematical, terms.

The high view of models places a higher value on the model's usefulness for continued explication. Since the model is a product of the human imagination it gives us only a partial view of dealing with reality, but it remains useful. The high view of models is like Barbour's critical realism and the low view is like his instrumentalism.

Sallie McFague's book is important because her feminist critique of theological models is combined with her description of how models are used in science. When this awareness is brought to theological discussion and combined with the political critiques by liberation theologians the total result gives theology a greater awareness of theological models and their limits as well as their promise.

A more open and flexible view of theological models helps prevent making idols out of models. A golden calf is easy to recognize as an idol, but the language by which idols are discussed can also become a subtle trap of self-reference.

Increased awareness about the use of models and the function of the other map-making tools, including paradigms, can aid us to compare the faith developmental models and paradigms of Fowler and Keen. To further aid in the comparison of the Fowler and Keen Models a short interpretation of the distinction between the use of models in science and in theology follows:

The Use of Models[8]

In Science

1. Models are grounded in theories which influence observations. Discordant data is often called an anomaly rather than a falsification. Paradigm shifts have as much to do with psychology as logic and data because of the paradigm's frame of reference.

2. Theory dominates in the form of laws rather than models.

3. Empirical testing is used to verify models.

4. No root-metaphor or original model is referred back to as a primary guiding image.

5. The purpose of models is to discover new phenom-

In Theology

1. Models are grounded in sacred stories (myths in the positive sense of being more than history) which are transmitted by a faith community and which inform human imagination with images and patterns for behavior. The sacred stories are enacted in rituals and involve gestures, drama and rites. The model is the enduring structural component which the myth dramatizes. The language system is given flexibility by its parable functon.

2. Models dominate theory. Doctrines such as creation and redemption are not translated into general laws.

3. Data neither falsifies nor verifies the truth value of models. The test is related more to the lives of exemplars and their ability to positively and creatively deal with the existential limits of life and ultimate value.

4. The root-metaphor of the personal deity relating to human beings and the natural world as the source and transformer of both is referred back to and is the primary guiding image.

5. The purpose of models is the comprehension of all reality to provide an or-

ena and explain how the modeled systems function.

dering and evaluating action from an ultimate perspective at the edge of being and knowing.

6. There are few models in science and they are not related hierarchically nor are they all complementary such as the wave and particle models of light are.

6. Many models are used in theology and they are related in complementary and hierarchical ways. The early church spoke of Christology for example in terms of "Son of Man," "the Word made Flesh," "Son of God," "Second Adam," and "Messiah" models.

7. Models can be translated into mathematical formulae which make general statements about relationships.

7. Models cannot be improved by translation into a different symbol system. For example one can say: "A was in B relating C asymmetrically to A." The relationships remain empty in this generalized form without the content of the model which is: "God was in Christ reconciling the world to Himself."

8. Relationships are primarily expressed in terms of quantity.

8. Relationships are primarily expressed in terms of quality.

9. Models primarily impact reason

9. Models primarily impact feelings.

Putting some of the characteristics of scientific and theological models side by side graphically raises questions about the relationship between their two paradigms. Since paradigms give models their framework of meaning it follows that whereas complementary models might exist within a single paradigm, there is little reason to think that paradigms can be complementary. Each paradigm is a view of reality with its own language and rules of logic which generate statements about the reality grounded in that viewpoint.

Ian Barbour stressed the sociological, historical, and epistemological power of paradigms in *Myths, Models and Paradigms* in 1974.[9] He defined a paradigm as a tradition transmitted through historical exemplars. This was based on Kuhn's statement in his 1970 version of his views. At that time he formulated the hallmarks of a paradigm's frame of reference in three points. The first point was that a paradigm was a research tradition. Secondly, it used key historical examples to transmit the tradition. Thirdly, a set of metaphysical assumptions were implicit in the fundamental conceptual categories.

Kuhn has revised his views during the continuing debate sparked by the first edition of *The Structure of Scientific Revolutions* in 1962.[10] By 1977 he had become more precise and limited in his view of paradigms.[11] His 1977 view was that paradigms are essentially a disciplinary matrix which includes three elements: "Symbolic generalizations," "models," and "exemplars." The symbolic generalizations are formal expressions such as mathematical formulae. The models are preferred analogues whether the preference is based on an instrumental or critical realism view of model status. The exemplars are concrete problem solutions.

The earlier and more general view of Kuhn provided Barbour with a comparison broad enough to enable him to say that religion and science do not differ in kind but only degree in the way they view reality. This makes a certain sense since the common denominator between them is the human imagination.

Our imagination is the *sine qua non* in every field of human intelligence. This still does not infer that science and religion are complementary in any formal sense. One, therefore, needs to be careful when working in the interface between religion and science to keep paradigm boundaries clear to avoid the logic and truth values of one paradigm being drawn into the other paradigm unawares to make a muddle rather than meaning. Perhaps it is fair to say that religion and science are not complementary, but they can cooperate in creative ways which are more powerful generators of meaning than either paradigm could be alone.

This brings our discussion of the cartographer's tools of symbol, metaphor, model, and paradigm to an end. We turn now to a discussion of the map-makers and their methods.

The Cartographer Factor

The history of map-making teaches us that one must be careful to select one's cartographer with care. It is not enough to pick the map most recently drawn. The great cartographer, Eratosthenes (d. 194 B.C.E.), who was a contemporary of Archimedes and directed the Great Library at Alexandria, was the best of his time. Another Alexandrian, Ptolemy, was an Egyptian astronomer and geographer who flourished about 127–151 C.E. His book, *Geography*, surpassed Eratosthenes and attempted to place geography on a formal and mathematical basis by using latitude and longitude.

The original maps of Ptolemy were destroyed in the burning of the Great Library in Alexandria by Christian zealots in C.E. 389. Wars and invasions in the West during the Middle Ages would have destroyed all remaining copies of his maps if they had not been saved and preserved by the Arabs.

During the time of the Roman Empire contacts with India and China had been frequent, but the trans-Asian routes had been closed to Europeans by the Islamic conquests of the seventh century. By the eleventh century the Arabs had expanded the world map to China in detail.

The situation in eleventh century Europe was that geographical knowledge had declined to cartography like that of the earliest Babylonian clay maps of the world from the sixth century B.C.E. The wheel map was used again in the West and the earth was imagined as flat. Now, however, the Mediterranean basin was placed at its center. The earth was ringed with water and near its center was the Mediterranean Sea.

The Arabs during this time showed a detailed knowledge of the routes to China which were unknown to the Europeans, but the Arabs did not know Northern Europe. Prejudice and a lack of first-hand travel distorted map-making in both East and West.

By the fourteenth century the magnetic compass was used for navigation. Sea travel could now be conducted beyond the sight of land. Charts became essential. Map-makers slowly learned to transmit facts instead of legend and dogma in maps.

A great map was drawn at the Benedictine monastery at Ebstorf in Germany in 1280. The physical world was drawn as the manifestation of Christ. The head, hands, and feet of Christ marked the four points of the compass. Jerusalem, the capital city of Christ's kingdom, is still at the center of the world. The Garden of Eden was given definite, terrestrial location along with more earthly geography.

It is important to choose a cartographer whose most detailed and familiar work coincides with where you want to go. Abraham Cresques, as we have said, gave the great Catalan Atlas compiled in Barcelona in 1375 to Charles VI of France. He not only included the earth but the heavens as well. His guide to the constellations connected all information in concentric circles of fantasy, but his map of the world was more grounded in material fact. Despite the details in the earthly map, however, it was Spain that was most correct. Even Northern Europe was distorted despite its relative closeness.

It is also good to have a cartographer who is honest. Columbus might be compared to a companion on his second trip, Juan de la Cosa, in this regard. Columbus was a traveling seller of old maps. He read all he could find about what ancient geographers had to say. He knew Eratosthenes, Strabo, and Ptolemy. When he "proved" his voyage would work, however, he had to cheat on his calculations as the faculty of the University of Salamanca correctly pointed out. He had used the smallest possible circumference of the earth he could find, the greatest eastward extension of Asia available, and still juggled his figures.

On his second voyage the men were made to swear a warrant that Cuba was not an island but a part of the mainland of Asia. The oath was necessary for commercial reasons to prove his assertion that the western route to India was shorter and cheaper. De la Cosa swore the oath.

In 1502 De la Cosa drew a map to guide sailors into the New World. He proved to be an honest cartographer and charted Cuba as an island. At the far western end of the map he, also, drew in a curved surface and made it appear to be the end of the earth. His honesty might have been a bit compromised by that bit of fantasy but he cannot be doubted as a true cartographer. He even included information received secondhand from Cabral about Brazil and from Cabot about Canada. He also included information about the coastlines of Africa and India gathered by Vasco da Gama, a Portuguese rival of Columbus, who had pioneered the expensive eastern route to India.

Charts were produced individually by hand and decorated with fantastic creatures and brilliant colors. All this was

done by experts and drafting was one of the foremost profes-
sions. After printing was developed these methods gave way
to wood-block engraving. Charts became black and white,
utilitarian products. Today with improved color printing
they have been somewhat restored to their former beauty
and now we have an accuracy informed by photographs
from outer space.

The cartographers of faith development use utilitarian
maps of black and white. The map-makers, Fowler and
Keen, both compile the best knowledge but it is gathered
in different ways. Their dreams and fears are not totally
excluded from the maps they have drawn, but they take
responsibility for these distortions. They are both involved
in the travel they chart. It is a detailed area they know.
They are honest and both desire to know what faith development truly is.

There is more than curiosity involved here. Both Fowler
and Keen work from a desire to know combined with an
element of fun. The journey dialogues back and forth with
the map-making. They both enjoy the chase, delight in the
chance, and involve themselves deeply in the creativity it
takes to do this work.

In the most important ways the cartographers, Fowler
and Keen, are much alike. A few words need to be said
about this since they appear to be so different in style and
method. To substantiate the assertion about their common
honesty and competence a few biographical notes need to be
added.

We will begin with geography. Both Fowler and Keen
have a bit of the Smoky Mountains in common. Fowler
grew up in western North Carolina in small towns such
as Spruce Pine, Bandanna, and Kona. Keen grew up in Mary-
ville, a town of about 10,000 people south of Knoxville,

in eastern Tennessee. Geographically, the Smoky Mountains stood between them.

Both Fowler and Keen grew up in Protestant families. Fowler's father was a Methodist minister and Keen's family had a conservative Presbyterian heritage. Both went east for their theological education and both went on to do graduate work at Ivy League schools. Fowler's Ph.D. is from Harvard and Keen's Ph.D. is from Princeton. Both became professors at theological seminaries related to their theological heritage. Fowler is now at Candler School of Theology which is Methodist and Keen served as Professor of Philosophy and Christian Faith at Louisville Presbyterian Theological Seminary. Both, however, bridged their theological training with another academic area. Fowler combined the social sciences with theology during his training and Keen combined philosophy with theology.

With these common characteristics in mind we can turn to the differences between the cartographers of faith in *Life Maps*. Their similarities make their differences even more interesting. We shall explore three broad areas. One is the difference in their style of conversation. A second difference is between their exemplars and their traditions. A third difference is between the methods which they use.

Fowler and Keen differ in style, because they are different people. They are on different journeys. Fowler is more academic and Keen is more attuned to conversation with a broader audience. On the other hand, Keen is read by academics, often with frustration, and Fowler is read by a broad audience, usually people interested in Christian education.

The academic setting in which Fowler works is at Candler School of Theology in Atlanta where he is a professor and directs the Center for Faith Development. The conversation which surrounds his work can be illustrated by several kinds of academic responses and interaction. There are Ph.D. theses of young scholars at important theological centers such as Harvard, Toronto, and Chicago.[12] There have been articles in religious education journals.[13] There have been reports in research publications.[14] There have also been references in foreign publications[15] and scholars from outside of the United States have come to the Center for study. Finally, there has been at least one book-length essay referring to Fowler's work. It was written by Gabriel Moran.[16] In addition to responses in publications there also has been a study sponsored by the Religious Education Association about adult faith development in the United States and Canada[17] which has used Fowler's model.

Sam Keen began in an academic setting, but after 1969, when he published *Apology for Wonder,*[18] he moved from being a professor to become what he has termed a "free-lance philosopher." His livelihood since then has depended on lectures, workshops, and the publication of articles and books. The magazine, *Psychology Today,* where he has been a consulting editor, was the main focus for his publishing activities for many years.

Fowler has also done workshops and public lectures in a variety of settings. When he began to put his research team together, he used to comment on the change he experienced in the shift from being a scholar working alone in the library or at his typewriter to being a team director. He has been a good research director and in addition has been a willing and perceptive mentor to many who have worked for him on the various faith development research projects.

Sam Keen has continued to work alone for the most part, but his way of working is not confined to the library and the typewriter. He writes out of his personal experience in contrast to the Fowler team approach. Both Fowler and Keen, however, take responsibility for their work and realize that their own journeys have much to do with what they have selected to study and observe.

The mentors of Fowler and Keen can be identified partially by their Ph.D. theses. Fowler's theological mentor, H. Richard Niebuhr, was the subject of his thesis. Fowler's primary research mentor was Jean Piaget and, perhaps, Erik Erikson — although he mentions Jung and others. His goal has been to discover the faith development structures by the developmental, structuralist approach.

Keen's Ph.D. thesis was about Gabriel Marcel, who was his mentor theologically and methodologically. Keen has attempted to uncover the structure of faith by means of the method of phenomenology. Both the developmental structuralist tradition and the tradition of phenomenology will be discussed now.

Piaget distinguished what he called "energetics" from cognition for purposes of research. Human feelings (energetics) provide motive force but cognition is of such importance that it is worthy to be separated out artificially for study.

This is not the place to distinguish the Piaget, Kohlberg, and Selman strands of the developmental structuralist tradition. One does need to note that they do use different methods of research and particular attention needs to be given to a major difference between Piaget and Kohlberg.

Piaget set up experiments which allowed the observer to watch children working with objects in the natural world, such as containers of liquid or rods of equal length that were moved into various positions. Guiding questions were used in a clinical interview to see how the children articulated their reasoning about what they did or observed about these objects.

Kohlberg used hypothetical dilemmas for his research. Moral judgment was studied as it operated on hypothetical dilemmas. The method logicians use to deal with dilemmas, breaking the horns of the dilemma and reframing the question, was not allowed to the subjects. As Kohlberg's research developed, the situations in the social world were made more concrete and relevant to children and adults, but they remained mainly hypothetical until Carol Gilligan asked pregnant women to reflect on their thoughts concerning abortion.[19]

Fowler also used Erik Erikson, at least in his theory building but perhaps also in his method. Erikson's developmental model was organized in cycles of the generations with eight inner cycles or stages within each generation. The stages were made up of pairs of salient life issues which needed to be resolved. They were stimulated by the environment and biological growth. A positive resolution of these pairs of critical issues resulted in strengths which were called "virtues" in *Insight and Responsibility*.[20] They are hope, will, purpose, competence, fidelity, love, care, and wisdom.

Erikson made little effort to be representative in quotations or be systematic with his references. His observations were of a "configurational" kind which involved observation combined with self-observation. He said his book, *Childhood and Society*,[21] which stated his developmental cycles, was a "subjective book, a conceptual itinerary." His research drew on his clinical experience with people in therapy. It included his historical studies of figures such as Luther and Ghandi. It also included his anthropological studies such as those with the Indians of America.

It is difficult to decide which of the seven aspects of a faith stage (please see pp. 39–41 for an overview of these seven aspects and pp. 96–99 for more details) flow out of which research traditions. One might speculate that all seven aspects of a faith stage are logic-related or, at least, reveal themselves in logical structure. They differ according to what object or objects the logical operation is performed on. In the three Piaget-related aspects (Piaget, Kohlberg, Selman) we find that the Piagetian research is primarily related to the natural world. In Kohlberg and Selman we find the focus primarily on the social world. The two identity-related or Erikson-related aspects might be considered to be the ones where the structures of logic operate on the range of social reference and one's relation to authority. The remaining two aspects are related to how logic operates on the ultimate environment to generate patterns of coherence and how one's use of symbols to compose an ultimate environment functions. These last two aspects of faith stage seem somewhat Jungian-related.

In *Life Maps* Fowler said, "Our work, on the other hand, is significantly indebted to the psychoanalytic and depth-psychology approaches used by Erikson and Jung" (p. 37). Just what that indebtedness is remains less than clear. He also said that the unconscious aspect of faith's structure must be distinguished from that of Jung and Erikson (pp. 136–137).

Piaget emphasized structures of thinking and Erikson stressed the ego and identity formation. Jung stressed the power of symbols to bridge and balance the unconscious and conscious forces at work in the integrated human being. Wallace B. Clift called symbols "channelizers of psychic energy."[22] It is this power that causes the symbols to be numinous, Jung theorized, and it is this channel through which the self-regulating system which maintains the equilibrium between the conscious and unconscious realities operates.

One might object to any suggestion that Jung's work with symbols is related to Fowler's work because Jung did not pay attention to developmental factors. It is true that Jung was not greatly interested in child psychology. A complete developmental model, however, has been constructed from Jungian writings and principles by Michael Fordham,[23] a London psychiatrist.

What is interesting is that if Jung's influence is to be found in Fowler's treatment of symbols and symbol systems, then, the use of Jung's method to gain access to one's symbolic functioning would be expected to be employed. It is not used to my knowledge although Fowler is very much aware of this approach. Fowler's method uses the guided clinical interview, but Jung employed dream interpretation, art, and guided imagination to evoke symbols which in turn were interpreted by retrospective or prospective means to see where symbols were not functioning well to maintain the balance between the unconscious and conscious realities.

As Fowler and his associates have worked with the faith development model and research, the integration of the model has taken place. The research traditions that flow into it have become re-framed into the Fowler guided interview which is described in *Stages of Faith*[24] in Appendix A. A scoring manual will be ready in 1985 and preliminary studies of inter-rater reliability have suggested that its use will be as high as 95–100 percent accurate.[25]

The variety of theoretical and methodological resources used by Fowler yield a rich, multi-perspective view of faith using seven aspects. These aspects have over time become a single model which is identified by Fowler's name. Like wave and particle models for light one might argue that we know more about faith by using all seven aspects than we do by arguing which one is most correct. On the other hand, can we say that "aspects" are complementary models if they are disconnected from their specific methodologies? I doubt that. What we have instead is the use of different traditions for theory building and the use of a single method for looking at these aspects of a faith stage. This causes us to ask whether it is faith being measured or a more elaborate and richer view of cognition, one that includes focusing on objects in the natural world, the social world, and one's ultimate environment?

There are many questions one might ask which can contribute to the continuing conversation. Perhaps, we should not leave this point without asking one more question. Do the aspects suggested by Fowler flow out of traditions which have the same end point? The end point most like Fowler's is that of Jung. Jung's approach spoke of the ability to use the uniting function of symbols to be aware of one's depth in the relationship within and with the outside environment. The sense of self that he develops is both centered and open, much like Fowler's description of his sixth stage.

The end point for Erikson is the strength of wisdom. He did not write extensively about this stage, but it appears that it is a detached and yet active concern with life itself in the face of death itself. An integrity of experience is present in spite of the decline of bodily and mental functions. This strength gives the ego and identity health during one's last days when a beneficial ratio of the positive ego integrity and the negative despair is accomplished.

The end point for Piaget was when the ability to perform the cognitive actions needed to use the scientific method were developed. Formal operations is a stage of cognitive maturity that develops as early as adolescence and gives one the structures by which to form a hypothesis and then test it. It is clear that this had to be extended into the three latter stages by Fowler for this relationship to the natural world to be able to fit with the other aspects of a faith stage.

The end point for Fowler's stages is one that moves beyond Piaget's stages and into the ability to use symbols in a special way to relate to one's ultimate environment. Perhaps the most critical operation needed to accomplish the last stage is the "postcritical rejoining of symbolic nuance and ideational content" (p. 99). He drew on Paul Ricoeur's concept of the "second naivete" and Paul Tillich's movement from the experience of existence to the experience of essence in "essentialization" to formulate this. It is also compatible with the shift that takes place in the Jungian developmental view of adults as well.

We turn now to the tradition of cartography of Sam Keen and his primary mentor, Gabriel Marcel (1889–1973). Marcel was a French philosopher, usually grouped with the existentialists. Keen's books often include at least one list of existentialists' names like a song of sacred heros. Such a litany evokes the struggle to know the truth and to be an authentic person for Keen.

The mosaic called existentialism was expressed in philosophical writing, plays, poetry, novels, and short stories. It was lived as a protest against rationalism, against people being reduced to things, against the split between person and what the person perceives, and especially against any easy solutions to the ambiguity of life by bad faith or cheap grace. Perhaps, existentialism was a corrective to philosophy and theology rather than a self-sufficient position, but what is certain is that within this group of people we find the philosophical matrix of Keen's journey.

Marcel was born in Paris. His mother and grandfather

died when he was very young and he was raised by his nurse, his aunt, and his grandmother. He was a brilliant pupil, winning most of the prizes, but he was repelled by that approach to life. During the First World War, as he worked in the Red Cross, he became suspicious of the spirit of abstraction. He also became suspicious of system building.

Another French Philosopher, Henri Bergson (1859–1941), had been known for antiintellectual sentiments. David E. Roberts, an early interpreter of existentialism and religious belief, noted that the relationship between Marcel and Bergson was based more on a common appreciation of intuition and creativity than their antiintellectualism.[26] Both Marcel and Bergson belong to the part of the French cultural tradition which is most at odds with the structuralists and mathematicians, the group to which Piaget's temperament was most closely aligned.

The existentialists and Marcel are not read as widely today as they were in mid-century. A good introduction to Marcel's work is the collection of essays, *The Philosophy of Gabriel Marcel*,[27] which includes Marcel's replies to the scholars writing about him. In addition this volume includes Marcel's own appraisal and memory of his life. Among the articles about Marcel in this book is one by Sam Keen, finished in June of 1968. This complements his little book on Marcel published in 1967.[28]

Marcel was a free-lance writer, editor, critic, playwright, and lecturer. He was also a talented musician with an interest in experimental music. He maintained an interest in parapsychology and spiritualism both because of his personal experiences but also to guard against becoming trapped in the philosophical prejudice that the self was a closed, rational entity. He knew in addition that religious intersubjectivity was based on something that cannot be controlled by technique. He said that "The only genuine inward mutation is . . . inconceivable without . . . grace."[29]

Unlike Marcel, Keen sought to be employed as a professor after his graduate training. By 1969, his identity as a professor had fragmented. The book, *To a Dancing God*,[30] expresses some of that pain in 1970.

Keen went West to prospect for grace in California. He moved away from his first marriage, his father's death in 1964, from Presbyterian seminaries, and from his roots in the hills. He moved toward Esalen, politics, and a call for the reformation of theological and general education. He was asking, "Is there anything in my experience which gives it unity, depth, density, dignity, meaning and value — which makes graceful freedom possible?"[31]

Marcel's image of the *Homo Viator*, the Wayfarer, probably identifies Keen's vision of what a philosopher is. He seemed to love and hate the notion of an academic career, but he was fully in agreement with Marcel who said that "The imperishable glory of a Kierkegaard or a Nietzsche consists . . . mainly in this, that they have proved . . . by their trials and by their whole life, that a philosopher worthy of the name cannot be a man of congresses, and that he deviates from his path every time that he allows himself to be torn from the solitude which is his calling."[32]

The style of life as *Homo Viator* is similar in both Keen and Marcel although details of their family life were much different. Their writing style was also more alike than different. Marcel refused to write systematic works. His books consisted of journal entries, essays or lectures. Even the two volumes of his Gifford Lectures, published as *The Mystery of Being*,[33] seem built up from meditations and more like poetry than most academic philosophy.

Keen's style did not fit into the canons of scholary communication any more than Marcel's did, but there was a brief moment when he was in style during an enthusiasm about autobiographical theology. Despite a lack of general academic acclaim his books have always sold well.

Keen's views on story are often overlooked today because they were expressed before that wave of interest crested and because his ideas are tucked away in several uneven books. The one complete volume on story was built up from his workshops and published with Anne Valley Fox. *Telling Your Story*[34] was published in 1973 and it was dedicated to "the outlaws among us who are living their own stories."

Today Keen writes of a place beside a waterfall. The horses stamp and steam in the cool of the morning and an "ancient cottonwood shades the glen." His place is where a giant climbed the impossible tree to put up the "paradisical swing." The new child, Keen, you, and I can for a moment swing out, as he writes of it, "Over the valley, over the stream, over the years."[35] Like Marcel, Keen enjoys the rhythm and sound of words.

Keen's method is phenomenology. Many existentialists and especially Edmund Husserl (1859–1938) stand in the background of any discussion of this approach to the description of reality. Martin Heidegger had studied with Husserl and succeeded him at Freiburg. Jean Paul Sartre attended Husserl's lectures and studied with Heidegger. In 1934 Paul Ricoeur discovered both Husserl and Marcel in the same year.

The relationship between Husserl and Marcel is an interesting one. Ricoeur analyzed this relationship in an article in *The Philosophy of Gabriel Marcel.*[36] Marcel thanked him and responded to what Ricoeur described as the Husserl and Marcel connection by noting that there were similarities as well as an "abyss that separates us." To clear up any suggestion of influence, he said that "I am barely acquainted with Husserl's philosophy." He did recall reading the *Ideen* some months before the beginning of the First World War and "not understanding a word of it." He later read *Logical Investigations* and attended Husserl's lectures at the Sorbonne. "At first I found them interesting, then tiresome," he said.

Husserl has become somewhat of a cult figure. In *Voices and Visions*[37] Keen tells the story about a student of Husserl giving a piece of ebony that once stood on Husserl's writing desk to Carlos Castaneda. Castaneda gave it to Don Juan. "Don Juan fondled the ebony, as Husserl had done a generation before, and gave it an honored place in his treasury of power objects that are used for conjuring."

How did Keen use phenomenology? Edward Farley's book, *Ecclesial Man,*[38] includes a study of Husserl. He draws the distinction between those who use the phenomenological method(s) and the phenomenological attitude. Paul Ricoeur is included in Farley's list of those who use the method as well as "perhaps Erik Erikson."

It is difficult to say whether Keen uses the attitude or the method of phenomenology. In *Life Maps* there is not a formal and explicit use of the method and yet in his *Apology for Wonder*[39] the method is used.

In *Apology* Keen begins with a phenomenological description of wonder. Its object aspect revealed the kinds of wonder such as the ontologic, mundane, sensational, and familiar types. The characteristics these types of wonder have in common were discovered to be contingency, mystery, and presence. When Keen turned to the subjective aspect of the phenomenon, he described the stimulus as surprise, puzzlement, ambivalence, and admiration. The variety of responses to the stimulus of wonder are pathological when they seal off the ego from change or cause one to live in continual openness. The healthy response to wonder and its integration involve curiosity and explanation, contemplation and celebration. Finally, Keen compared wonder to a near "neighbor," the experience of the holy. He found them to be very much alike.

In his first book, *Gabriel Marcel,*[40] in 1967 Keen described the distinction Marcel made between primary and secondary reflection. The method requires one to bracket out primary reflection which deals in objectification, problems, abstraction, and I-it relationships. The method uses secondary reflection to participate in the phenomenon to know it from the inside by means of intersubjectivity. Once the relationship is properly established the objective and the subjective aspects of the relationship become clear, their structure emerging on its own terms rather than having one imposed upon it.

This approach is very different from what Piaget's method was like. His book, *Insights and Illusions of Philosophy,*[41] was devoted to attacking the idea that philosophy could generate a "superscientific knowledge."

Piaget discussed Merleau-Ponty, Sartre, Husserl, Jaspers, and others to distinguish between philosophical and scientific truth. Philosophical truth for him was a kind of "wisdom" which gives meaning to existence by ordering values rationally and by raising questions which go beyond "actual knowledge" (scientific truth). Wisdom is not intellectualist for Piaget, however. It is a means by which one can take a vital position.

Piaget's view of phenomenology is that the phenomenon is internal to consciousness. It is primitive and immediate, but this changes nothing at all. A primitive datum can be less true and more deceptive than an elaborated one. The belief that intuition is true because it is at one and the same time connected with that to which the intuition is directed is false, he says. Such an essence is both a concept of the subject and the phenomenal nucleus of the object. One still must submit the object to epistemological critique to know if the essence is true.

Piaget argues that the overcoming of a dualism of subject and object operates in science as well as in phenomenology. The observer and the observed are always modifying each other. The difference between science and phenomenology is that science progresses despite its crises and dead ends. It can do this because its thinking and observation are explicit and open to common investigation and agreement. Philosophy is not able to progress and remains locked in a certain number of almost permanent positions because it places too high a value on intuitions and not enough value on observation and critique.

Piaget investigated the changes in the patterns of cognition that result from the interaction of the person and the environment. The phenomenologist describes the relationship by entering it. This relationship provides the substratum upon which Piaget's interaction takes place. If the fiduciary relationship were not there, no cognition would be possible. In other words, Piaget assumes what the phenomenologist is studying while the phenomenologist attempts to bracket out what Piaget is studying.

Marcel wondered if the phenomenon of faith is the kind of entity that requires stepping into the relationship to know it. Perhaps, it must be known from the inside by fidelity. Fidelity is not the inertia of conformism. It is not merely an emotional or volitional act. It is the act of the whole person being available to the other through intersubjectivity.

The mystery present in the other reveals something permanent in the other. It is not life, but being.

The object of fidelity is being. The unconditionality of fidelity expresses the Absolute Thou and faith results when fidelity is pledged to God, the Absolute Thou. The faith relationship is so fundamental that we cannot get outside of it to know it or anything else. To know it, however, we must enter it and bracket out the ordinary ways of knowing to become aware of it as mystery rather than a focal problem to be studied.

Keen says in his article in *The Philosophy of Gabriel Marcel*[42] that Marcel trys to move in a middle ground between phenomenology and psychology when he attempts to know and describe fidelity and faith. Perhaps, we can say that the study of faith is also related to the study of being, and being is related to one's deepest identity, so the psychology of identity may be related to the phenomenological analysis of being and be a way to understand it best.

The difference of opinion between Piaget's view of the scientific method and his interpretation of phenomenology is somewhat dated now. Science today is more aware of how paradigms define facts and problems. The pull of systems such as the academic community or political networks create distortions Piaget did not comment on when he proposed that science prevents individual bias by using a spirit of cooperation and verification by many co-workers. Piaget's suspicion about existentialism's view of the reality of individual freedom was also well taken, but the power of systems on individual freedom is also something taken into account now.

Perhaps, what Piaget was really studying with the scientific method was how we think *about* the object we are interacting with. What Marcel and Keen studied by the phenomenological method is how to *enter* into relationship with the other and how the quality of that relationship can change both the subject and object poles of the relationship. In any case the depth of the difference between Fowler and Keen in terms of method has been suggested. We turn now to the next section which is to discuss the maps themselves.

Mapping the Journey As Development

The shape of the journey and the shape of the map are related. They interact. The great world map drawn in 1280 at the Benedictine monastery at Ebstorf, Germany, was round. It joined the spiritual and geographical journey. The map drawn by Juan de la Costa in 1502 was rectangular except at the end where the New World was drawn. A smooth curve there gave credence to the conviction of Columbus that the earth was round. The map drawn in 1546 by Pierre Desceliers, a priest from a town south of Dieppe, for Henry II of France, was 9 feet by 3 feet. It was designed to be laid on a table and read from both top and bottom. The usefulness of the size and lettering gave the representation of the land mass of North America reality despite its blur of speculation. It was peopled with pictures of confident Indians and confused Europeans in the interior, but it was a place to start one's journey in any case.

In our time the mapping of faith journeys are shaped as "development." Faith is the means by which we relate to our ultimate environment. The change in faith is related to a stable measurement by which the change can be identified. The story of the image of development and the relation of humankind to the ultimate environment can help furnish us with more perspective on the maps of faith we draw today. This story is the main part of this section. Development is at least a place to start mapping one's journey like Desceliers' map did.

Before turning to the story of the image of development, two preliminary matters will be helpful to consider. One is the use of the word, "development," today. The other is to speculate briefly on the different shapes the pattern of development might take. We turn first to the definition of "development."

The definition of the word, "development," has both a general meaning and specific meanings which depend on their context for their uniqueness. The general meaning carries the sense of being the opposite of the verb, *"en*velope." To *de*velop is to remove a covering, such as an envelope. It is also the act of unfolding, emerging, unrolling, or unwrapping.

The specific contexts which give special meanings to the word adjust the general meaning to their needs. In geometry development means to unbend a curved surface to make a flat one, as in the construction of maps. In mathematics a development is an expansion of any expression into an equivalent value or meaning. In photography one develops a photograph from the darkness of the negative. In music a development is the unfolding of a theme by modifications of melody, harmony, and beat. In economics an increase in quantity is development. In architecture a housing development is the actualization of what was drawn on the plans.

The space and time between the point of unfolding and the end-point of the development stretch out into some sort of pattern. The question of what that pattern's possibilities are is, perhaps, an endless one. But we need to consider some basic possibilities to give this part of the development the same attention as the beginning and ending points. Such a discussion is difficult without photographs. To enjoy such a discussion in pictures the reader is referred to Chapter 2 of Horace Freeland Judson's book, *The Search for Solutions*. [43]

We will deal here only with some basic shapes for pattern and dimensions that are easily visualized. If the pattern of development between the beginning and ending point is a single dimension, then we will talk of lines. Some lines will be considered to ascend and others to descend. Broken lines can rise and fall. Curved lines can indicate waves. Lines that cross over themselves begin to suggest two dimensional space.

When we add a second dimension the lines become figures on a plane. The lines might become squares and the curved lines might become circles. The squares and circles might be placed inside each other to make a nesting of squares and concentric circles. Motion might be suggested by this method as if a stone had been thrown into a pond to make concentric circles moving outward from the point of impact. Inverted triangles are an ancient shape that makes a six-pointed star.

When a third dimension is added the nesting squares become boxes and the circles become spheres. The six-pointed star becomes two inverted cones, much like Fowler's suggestion to illustrate his stage six (p. 134). In the realm of three-dimensional shapes we also have organic images of change.

The tree of life might be rooted in either the sky or the earth. The seed secretly growing or the sower sowing seed in a variety of soils are other organic images. Leaven enlivens change and becomes part of it. The child born to give birth to children touches infinity.

Space, time, and the shape of the journey restrict maps

and our imaginations. Sometimes we are trapped by our images and other times old patterns are seen in new ways to create new patterns for change. The story of the image of development is itself a story of change, or if you will, a story of the development of that image. It is a story that involves the human imagination playing with the confinement of permanence and change fixed into patterns and related to faith and the ultimate environment of humankind over time.

This story will begin with a stone ramp against a stable background upon which angels move up and down. It will continue to include ladders used by human beings. The next cosmic image was like an egg with the earth as its yoke. It lasted from about the second to the sixteenth century. The Copernician crack in the cosmic egg was completely shattered in the seventeenth century and could not be put back together again. It was replaced by Newton's machine of the heavens and earth run by gravity. In the nineteenth century everything was sensed as moving, even the human species. In our time we live in systems to conceptualize this multifarious movement and when one part of a system is touched reverberations are sensed throughout.

Our story begins with Jacob's Ladder (Genesis 28:12). In the Genesis account the Hebrew word translated as "ladder" is *sullām*. It is from the verb, *sālal,* which means "to heap up." Gerhard Von Rad speculated in his commentary, *Genesis,* [44] that this word indicated a heap of rocks such as those found in the ramps leading upward to the top of the ancient terraced pyramids called ziggurats. The Assyrians and Babylonians thought they literally connected heaven and earth.

The angels in Jacob's dream were ascending and descending the ramp. All else was fixed. Jacob marked the spot of his dream with a stone and dedicated it to God. Von Rad suggested that this place had its great period of pilgrimage about 926 B.C.E., but during "the first half of the second millenium Israel's ancestors came in contact with this sanctuary." This was clearly an ancient site and its importance was that here humankind was connected with the ultimate environment, God.

Other ancient peoples used more customary ladders for celestial movement. One might climb from the grave up into the world of the dead if one had the means. Little ladders were buried in Egyptian tombs to help the dead with their climb. People from Plato to Philo spoke of ladders.

The ancient words for "ladder" have come into English with meanings related to development. We get the word, "climax," from the Greek word for ladder. The Latin word for ladder gave us another developmental image, "scale." Roman pagan piety held that a soul ascended through the spheres of heaven upon death. It developed from the body's envelope.

Before turning to the Christian use of the image of development, we need to be reminded that change and permanence were related in other ways. Heraclitus of Ephesus (c. 536–470 B.C.E.) used the river. He observed that one never steps twice in the same river. It is always moving on. Fragments found of his writing propose that nothing is real except change and the only order is a succession of events.

In other parts of the world different images were used, but we will confine ourselves to a few Western images. In the East the presence of change, decay, and suffering stimulated the imagination to assume that this was only of surface importance. Reality had more to do with living in different forms and a movement toward life without being reborn into another form.

The link between the earth and heaven which Christ

showed was like a relationship between a son and a father. St. Paul shifted this focus a bit to say that the link is through identity with Christ. To be "in Christ" is to be linked to one's ultimate environment.

We change in the way we are with the Father or in Christ, so we need to resort to an image of development. The ladder again became important. In the fourth century Gregory of Nyssa used the image as did the Desert Fathers. In the fifth century Dionysius, the pseudo-Areopagite, did as well. His writings were translated into Latin from Greek and continued to have an influence on the whole of Europe, especially during the Middle Ages.

In the seventh century John Climacus (c. 570–649) was called "John of the Ladder of Paradise" because of his famous treatise which used the image of the ladder. The ladder of spiritual ascent or development had thirty rungs to recall what he thought were the thirty years of Jesus' life.

The Greek Aristarchus had held that the planets orbited about the sun, but in Greek astronomy the geocentric theory won out. Ptolemy, the author of the already mentioned *Geography*, also wrote a classic known by its Arab name, *Almagest*, "the Greatest." It summarized the ancient world's knowledge of astronomy and established the earth-centered view of the ultimate environment for 1,400 years until Copernicus.

The geocentric universe of Ptolemy was pictured and assumed in the *Divine Comedy* of Dante (1265–1321) where the search for blessedness began when the author was lost in a wood on Good Friday in 1300. The Inferno, Purgatory, and Paradise merged cosmology and geography with the spiritual journey.

The ladder remained important as an image, however. Walter Hilton (c. 1396) was an Augustinian canon. He wrote the *Scale of Perfection,* the "scale" being a ladder, in the four-teenth century without getting involved in geography or astronomy.

The visualized world of the Middle Ages mixed Ptolemaic, Aristotelian and biblical assumptions into a magnificent and satisfying "correlation of space and destiny."[45] One ascends toward heaven and God and descends toward eternal fires and Satan. The heavens were incorruptible dwelling places of the redeemed and of God. Hell was the place of suffering. The site of the ledges of Purgatory was thought to be some-where in the southern hemisphere.

In the sixteenth century the great correlation began to be cracked. The suggestion that the earth was round had not disturbed the immutable arrangement. Change was still located in human beings and their search for blessedness was played out against a stable background.

The old map died slowly. During the first step from Co-pernicus to Galileo there was no compelling reason to accept or reject the new ideas about the sun-centric universe. Be-tween Galileo and Newton it was still possible to enter-tain alternative positions, but the weight of the evidence was in favor of the new Copernican view. The third step was the domination of the Newtonian world-view.

The heavens had opened up and were in chaos. People had no way to get their bearings. The anxiety engendered by infinity and change related to the new world-view was increased by the apparent conflict between the Book of Scripture and the Book of Nature.

The quarter of a century, 1580–1605, in England was de-scribed by E. M. W. Tillyard[46] as a time when people were "hovering between equivalence and metaphor." The Eliza-bethan world-view conceived of the universe as a synthesis in three main forms: a chain, a series of corresponding planes above each other, and a dance.

The great chain is a very old image. In the *Illiad* (viii) of Homer, Zeus told the gods that he holds heaven and earth, including them on a giant chain, and that at any time he can pull them up into himself. This chain was later called "the vast chain of being" by Pope (1688–1744) in his *An Essay on Man* (line 237). The Elizabethan version of the great chain connected the smallest of inanimate objects to the foot of God's throne. It was also a kind of ladder since a progression was possible through the chain and in human beings which was a movement toward God.

The planes of existence and the cosmic dance were of less importance as images. The highest horizontal plane was God. Then there was the macrocosm, then the body politic, and then humankind summing up the universe in itself. The different levels influenced each other although it is not clear how one moved from one to the other.

The cosmic dance was a mixture of equivalence and metaphor as well. When the queen and her court danced one could literally see the power of the crown and the church dance a dance of political and religious embodiment in the realm. The cosmic dance kept the earthly, celestial, divine hierarchies, and God separate — but all danced in their place to make up the whole cosmos dancing together.

By the time Galileo died in 1642 it was clear that the earth was not a still point about which the perfect heavens turned. Imperfect objects could be seen in the celestial realms through telescopes, such as ones that Galileo himself made. Not everyone dared to look.

In the same year that Galileo died Isaac Newton was born on Christmas day. His imagination presented a new image of order and change by which to relate humankind to the ultimate environment. Gravity worked on earth and in the heavens as well. The ordered way mass particles acted on each other by impact and the way gravitational attraction worked joined all in a great machine, a sort of celestial clock of time and space. The new correlation was not between space and destiny as one's spiritual journey but between space and destiny as ordered by science. Science was considered to be objective, mechanistic, materialistic, and deterministic by the time the seventeenth century closed.

The human being still had a place to stand, however, in this Newtonian world. It was the standpoint of the observer. A dualism of mind and body, formulated by Descartes in this century (1596–1650) was established by his death at mid-century. This Cartesian distinction also led to the separation of reason and faith in this century to save religion from reduction to either reason or natural law.

The role of imagination began to shrink. Many parts of the old geocentric view of the universe were compartmentalized to force a rigid sense of order despite new ideas. Between 1640–1690 theology, for example, made a conscious effort to remove "metaphorical language from its professional discussion." Sallie McFague has noted that theology in this period attempted to be "pruned of ambiguity, imagery, repetitions, and contrasts."[47]

In the eighteenth century imagination in science and religion was more confined. There was no way to invent a larger frame of reference in which they might converse again. God was almost completely banished from the natural world and another dualism, the split of spirit and matter, was added to the Cartesian split of subject and object from the century before. God's only function was to set the cosmic clock in motion.

The seventeenth and eighteenth centuries confined imagination to poetry. Reason was limited to logic, philosophy and the sciences. The use of the Bible became very literal and people had faith in the Book itself as a fact record in competition with the facts of nature. Competition between religion and science focused on who possessed the ultimate and complete map of reality. Ironically, the very Book which had warned against Idolatry now became a graven image itself which was worshiped by many as an end in itself.

Movement began to challenge peoples' thinking even more as they approached the nineteenth century. By the late eighteenth century history included the image of development. Gibbon's great book, *The Decline and Fall of the Roman Empire,* described "the triumph of barbarism and religion." Development for that author was a process of decline from the classical high point of culture. Religion was mainly to blame for this negative development.

Human imagination transformed the cosmic egg of antiquity into the celestial machine as an image of ultimate reality. The eggshell had become confining rather than comforting and broke up. In the nineteenth century human imagination began to work again to replace the mechanical image of the ultimate environment that had in turn become too suffocating for the human spirit.

The nineteenth century valued the role of the imagination in broader ways than the previous two centuries. The Romantics came into the foreground in literature. Theology became more open. Theology and science began to speak to each other for a moment again, but a new shock for the imagination approached. It was the image of evolution. Not only was the background for human change in motion now about the sun but humankind discovered its own species was involved in change along with the rest of the animal, plant, and mineral kingdom.

The idea of development began to pervade the thinking of people in many fields as evolution. In geology Sir Charles

Lyell (1779–1875), the Oxford-trained geologist and naturalist, wrote about the development of the earth's crust. He influenced Darwin's view of evolution in person and by his writing.

Thomas Robert Malthus (1766–1834), the English clergyman and political economist, applied the idea of development to what he called "the dismal science" of economics. He wrote of the "struggle for existence" in a world of limited means. Both Alfred Russel Wallace and Charles Darwin applied this idea to the realm of biology.

The German philosopher, Georg W. F. Hegel (1770–1831), discovered a pattern in the history of culture that followed a development of a thesis, the emergence of an antithesis, and then the convergence of the two into a synthesis which in turn became a new thesis to keep the process moving.

Karl Marx (1818–1883) applied Hegel's pattern of change in the realm of ideas to the realm of economic realities. The Darwinian idea of the conflict between species in the struggle for existence within the natural order gave shape to Marx's central notion of the class struggle. He so admired Darwin that he asked permission to dedicate *Das Kapital* to the British scientist. Darwin refused.

A form of development different from Darwin's was presented by Henri Bergson (1859–1941), the French philosopher who was awarded the Nobel Prize for Literature in 1928. His view of change was that it was not an advancing scale. Neither was it a mechanical kind of adaptation.

Bergson saw change as the growing, evolving pattern of the life force which had no preconceived plan or law to guide its unfolding. It moved by trial and error but not in the way Darwin thought it did. Darwin's view did not allow for genuine novelty in the change, Bergson thought. He argued that the vital principle gropes forward, overcoming the obstacles put in its way by inert matter. It is self-directive.

The word, "groping," is relevant to Teilhard de Chardin's "mysticism of knowing" as well as to Bergson. Teilhard (1881–1955), the French Jesuit and scientist, had read Bergson's work, *Creative Evolution,* when it appeared in French in 1905. It cast doubt on a purely rational science and sought to connect mind and matter. It strove for a deeper explanation for the origin of life than mechanistic Darwinism.

Teilhard's word, "groping," acknowledges an extensive dependence on chance, but it also affirms that life has a direction, an orientation, a preference. As Thomas M. King, S. J. has pointed out in his study of Teilhard,[48] this developmental model might be called paradoxically "directed chance." The finality is present in life from the beginning. Life prefers increased life.

While many philosophers who focused on the process of life as development were not theists (Fichte, Schopenhaur, Nietzsche, Bergson, and others). Teilhard de Chardin was a Christian mystic. His mysticism was not that of unknowing, however, but of knowing. For him religion and science were two joined faces or phases of one and the same complete act of knowledge. God is to be found in the act of knowing.

The shock of losing another standpoint from which to relate faithfully to the ultimate environment shook many. The reaction against the view that the species was changing found a leader in the Anglican Bishop of Oxford, Samuel Wilberforce. At the historic meeting of the British Association which took place at Oxford on 30 June 1860, Wilberforce attacked evolution and Huxley defended it. The Bishop asked Huxley whether he was descended from an ape through his maternal or paternal grandfather and the debate descended to a level less than the best our species can offer in the way of fairness and intellect.

Darwin's *The Origin of Species* was first published in 1859. The United States was distracted by the Civil War, but a theological war of words and feelings began at mid-century and expanded as the decades continued. John Fiske, a lecturer in philosophy at Harvard, observed that the difficulty was that people had had their security systems challenged but that was not all. There was also a threat to the dignity of humankind and to the biblical cosmology, but that was not all. What bothered people most, he thought, was that evolution threatened the destruction of the natural theology which gave harmony and design to the world. The process of change in Darwin's theory chilled many because it seemed to shrink God's power to nothing.

The view that the earth as well as the species was in evolution was a challenge met by Archbishop Ussher. He said that God created fossils to test one's faith. They were not the remains of ancient creatures that no longer walked the earth.

In the United States Horace Bushnell became impatient with the details of the evolution controversy. He concluded that Genesis was mythic in character but he continued to be filled with the wonder of God's creation as he contemplated the process that science was uncovering.

Horace Bushnell (1802–1876) played a major role in using the developmental image for religion in the nineteenth century. He grew up in the Congregational Church and graduated from Yale Divinity School. His book, *Christian Nurture* (1847), developed the theory that Christian education should be based on gradual development. In his view, this was the way faith naturally grew. He rejected the idea that children should be assumed to be morally depraved until they experienced a vivid and specific conversion, usually at a revival meeting. The counterattack by the revivalistic view said that Bushnell removed the action of the Holy Spirit from his theory and reduced Christianity to a religious naturalism.

In the twentieth century the image of development as it related to Christian education was revived by George Albert Coe of Union Theological Seminary in New York. His book, *A Social Theory of Religious Education* (1917), raised the new question about whether faith development and transformation might be compatible.

The twentieth century has been a period when not only the species but also individuals in the human species have been viewed as being in process. It now seems as if everything is moving with a dizzy speed so that it is hard to get one's bearings in both science and religion.

The sense that everything is in the process of change, including the person making the observation, has given rise to two interesting developments. One is that the role of the imagination has been consciously enlarged in our deliberations and, second, this has prompted the awareness that one must show how his or her theory fits into the larger system and history of human model-building and map-making.

The expansion of the role of the imagination began because of science's interest in models and its awareness of its own history. In theology the changes in science were noted. In addition the awareness of linguistic and systems critiques created a climate in which theology and science could be more open and flexible when they discussed the use of models and spoke to each other across the boundary of their paradigms.

Today the image of development is shifting again. It is

moving from the closed system model of the machine which was useful in physics or in such systems as mixing chemicals in a container. In closed systems the eventual state is always determinable from the initial conditions. This is useful for experiments, but the open system is closer to the way reality and the ultimate environment are understood today where everything is moving, including the person making the observations.

An open or living system exists only through continual exchanges with the environment. Living, open systems are self-regulating as are closed systems, but in addition there is a continual inflow and outflow. There are two basic types of exchange with the environment. One is the exchange of energy and the other is the exchange of information. Open and living systems organize themselves in and through these two exchanges.

One additional note should be added concerning the use of systems thinking. Each system usually has a subsystem made up of component parts and their relations. Beyond the system focused on there usually is also a suprasystem to be kept in mind. Systems analysis is as if the great chain had returned in new language and with the movement of the cosmic dance joined with it. Each level of analysis highlights some phenomena and obscures others, so one's point of view, as it is changed, and what its focus is, can be kept in mind by this approach.

The modern version of systems thinking can be located, perhaps, by pointing to Ludwig von Bertalanffy, a Viennese professor of biology who emigrated to Canada in 1949. When he died in 1971 he was nominated for the Nobel Prize. There are many converging interests which have combined to make up what is called here "systems thinking." Among those who have contributed greatly to this view are Norman Weiner in cybernetics, Anatol Rapoport in game theory, Heinz Werner in psychology, and Claude Shannon in communications.

Our story is not yet over, however. There is one more very important point to make. Today the emphasis is on the development of the individual who is a participant and creator in living systems. The modern interest has been especially involved with the development of children but more recently this concern has shifted to adult development and how males and females differ in their development. This is an important ending to our story not only because such development has been somewhat overlooked in the past, but also because adult development theory is richly involved with the definition of the ending-point of the developmental point of view.

Life Maps, as we have said, resulted from a colloquium held in 1975. Interest in adult development was stirring. A major step which brought this discussion into the public consciousness was the 1976 publication of Gail Sheehy's book, *Passages.* [49] Her chatty and rapidly paced stories of people moving through life created a wide readership for such a topic.

The next year, 1977, the more scholarly works began to appear in print. George Vaillant published his report on an all-male study begun in the 1940s. The sample was narrow. It was made up of men who had graduated from Harvard. The book was called *Adaptation to Life.* [50]

In 1978 Daniel Levinson published his book, *The Seasons of a Man's Life.* [51] His sample was broader than the Harvard one, but although this latitude in socioeconomic terms was present the sample was still all male.

Transformations [52] was published by Roger Gould in 1978 as well. He had studied men and women who were patients

and nonpatients in his sample to discover what preoccupations were specific to each age group. He distinguished these
specific preoccupations from general ones such as anxiety
and depression which were common to all ages.

This year, 1978, was also the year that Bernard Boelen
published his book, *Personal Maturity*.[53] He proposed ten
stages and grounded his work in existentialist philosophy.
Both Gould and Boelen ended their development theories
about the age of fifty years. Although Gould worked from
a psychoanalytic model and Boelen worked from an existentialist one, they both left open what a person becomes after
reaching the ideal state of being rational, independent, pro-
ductive, and efficient.

Gabriel Moran's critique of this literature is important.
His book, *Religious Education Development: Images for the Future*,[54]
argues that these studies are both sexist and ageist. Neither
women nor old people fit comfortably into the maps thus
far mentioned. With Erik Erikson he asks, what does life
move toward? Is it "an adulthood in which rationality and
independence are situated within a childlike attitude, or else
a childishness after one is no longer certified as an
adult?"

There is some literature about human development which
is less sexist and ageist than those previously mentioned.
One might for example cite the work of Bernice Neugarten[55]
in which she points out that most of our theories of development are still "childomorphic." The compelling issues of
adult life such as work, love, time, and death are not usually
considered among the main issues.

The work of Marjorie Lowenthal is also of note. Her
book, *Four Stages of Life*,[56] was published in 1976 and included
essays on human development. Her conclusion is that men
and women develop in some ways the same and in other

ways differently. This seems like common sense, but the important point is that research has borne this out.

Carol Gilligan, whom we have mentioned before, has probably done the most important and widely read study concerning the difference between men and women in the way that moral judgments are made. Her book, *In a Different Voice*,[57] was published in 1982 and was based on her study of women making judgments about their own pregnancy and the possibility of abortion. She had noticed that Kohlberg's work was initially based on a sample of seventy-two men in the 1950s and that the dilemma questions had males as the key role players. She also noticed that women seemed to score consistently lower than males on his scales. Her work has helped correct gender distortions which had become part of moral development studies.

Fowler has been sensitive to the bias of white males in his work and the men and women on his research teams have helped him monitor this. Keen's situation is more difficult. Since he is working in the laboratory of his own white male experience and because he usually is working alone, it has been difficult to bracket out this predisposition when investigating faith development or the stages of loving.

Keen identified the most critical point in gender awareness to be the breaking away from the stereotype of "normality" by the "outlaw" who goes beyond stereotypes to demythologize them. In *The Passionate Life*[58] he counsels that this can be done by embracing what each sex fears the most. According to his experience this is impotence for men and frigidity for women. When this embracing is done the outlaw can declare the war between the sexes to be at an end and reclaim the opposite sex as friends.

This brings us to the question of how these studies of adult maturity define the end-point of their developmental model. Fowler tends to be descriptive until he reaches the end-point. In the last stage his reliance on evidence declines and he presents the names of persons whom the reader is expected to know and, furthermore, to know what they have in common that identifies this structure of this last stage. In *Life Maps* a single case is presented (pp. 90–95). In *Stages of Faith* no case is presented for this stage. This suggests that while the earlier stages are descriptive generalizations from evidence, the final stage is more normative or prescriptive.

Keen is unambiguous about his approach being normative. In *The Passionate Life*[59] he says that his normative judgments are based on his own "impediments to love . . . blind alleys, and procrustean beds." The portrait he presents there of "the complete lover" is not as a philosophical self-portrait, but is an effort "to gain a glimpse of the hope that lures me toward becoming myself."

This brings our story and this section to a close. We began with Jacob's ladder and have ended with the ladders of adult development, males and females being distinguished. At the beginning, change was the angels going up and down. Today all is in movement, including the male and female cartographers. This modern situation has made it necessary for those who present developmental maps to speak more personally about how their maps relate to this story of developmental maps and where the new map fits into the modern scene. Two examples will show such awareness already at work. One example is from religious education and the other is from science.

Gabriel Moran's book, *Religious Education Development*,[60] is 226 pages long, including the notes. There are 126 pages which evaluate developmental theory from moral development to Fowler's faith development. This means that a little over half of the book was devoted to situating the proposed developmental theory in the context of other relevant models.

The same sort of awareness is present in science. Jerome Kagan's book, *The Nature of the Child*,[61] was written with the historical context in mind. He said that the themes he selected in child development to write about were picked because of his interest and experience, but also they were picked to "repair an imbalance." They are themes that despite early popularity in the century are neglected today.

It is of more than passing interest to notice that Kagan's book discusses the image of the journey. He wrote that in his judgment this is an inappropriate image for development because there is more discontinuity than previously thought in the way a child moves through the sequence of stages. He counsels us to have a skeptical attitude toward any strong form of connectedness between the distant past and the present in human development.[62]

We conclude this section with Kagan's warning about the image of the journey and its relation to development. We turn now to the last section. It is concerned with gaining perspective on the maps presented in this book in a way that includes one's own faith map.

Mapping Faith Maps

There are many ways to gain perspective. One way is to present the matter as closed. Another way impedes closure and works indirectly to contribute to a continuing conversation and a later but richer closure. The plan here is to pursue the latter course. This means that the last section of this chapter will be Socratic at best and indirect at least.

The plan is to raise questions first about what this book,

Life Maps, is like. Two other books which contribute to perspective in their fields, the study of the mind and the study of communication, will be presented and compared to *Life Maps*.

The second question asks how Fowler and Keen relate to the ancient controversy between faith and reason. Some of the "historical echoes" alluded to in the Introduction to *Life Maps* (p. 2) will be made explicit.

The third question asks what the reader's faith map is like. Is it more like Fowler's or Keen's in terms of the tools used, the cartographer factor, and the developmental image's usefulness; what does the movement to a position beyond the Fowler, Keen, and the reader's personal model contribute to understanding all three?

It is the intent, as was expressed at the beginning of this chapter, to keep the conversation going beyond the pages of this book. It was not primarily a sense of humor or a sense of irony that prompted the editor to engage the authors in the *Life Maps* conversation. It was the intuition that they represented major and radically different positions in the faith discussion. It was hoped that their interaction would relate these opposing positions in new and creative ways and, thus, move the discussion forward to new discoveries. You, the reader, must be part of this process. We turn now to the first question. What is this book like?

More than taxonomy is involved here. This is not a guidebook to classify faith development models like butterflies or beetles might be arranged in the glass case of a museum. Faith is difficult to classify and study because it is an aspect of life so close to the fundamental definition of what it is to be human. It is very difficult to stand back from faith to analyze it without losing a sense of what it is. It is like using the mind to think about the mind or communicating about communication. This is why books from these two areas will be presented briefly for comparison with our interest in faith.

Charles Hampden-Turner published *Maps of the Mind*[63] in 1981. He said that the book was necessary because maps are like shadows, a two-dimensional representation of a three-dimensional object. The shift from three to two dimensions distorts the object and limits the observer to a single point of view. One can compensate partially for the single point view and the distortion by presenting many points of view.

Maps of the Mind presents sixty pictures and discussions of mind models grouped into nine levels. The levels range from narrower to broader conceptions of mind and from earlier to later views historically. The image Hampden-Turner used to describe the book was putting Humpty-Dumpty together again.

The picture-discussion presentations are like snapshots of models of the mind. The brief text and striking illustrations capture salient aspects of each model so they can be compared.

The only process described by the book is a line of historical development which shows the struggle to gain freedom from repressive gods and from the suffocating mechanical laws of Newtonianism. The mind's rich awareness of itself becomes clear and is especially celebrated by the book.

The only attempt at synthesis is in Map 60, "Ecology or Catastrophe." It focuses on evaluation. The author says, "human beings perceive, speak, symbolize and process information in bimodal patterns while moral judgments tend to fasten obsessively on one of two modes." He calls for a new way to make value judgments and offers a proposal. "When value judgments are enacted, they either increase the salience and synergy of the elements in the value system or they split and diminish those elements. We can measure, observe, or otherwise estimate such growth or regression." The test for virtue or vice is, therefore, empirical and pragmatic. An ecological, co-evolutionary relationship with the environment is preferred rather than one of attempted conquest, the backlash from which produces catastrophe.

The second book is about communication. Richard W. Budd and Brent D. Ruben edited *Interdisciplinary Approaches to Human Communication*[64] and published it in 1979. The purpose of the book was to help deal with a perceived fragmentation and lack of coordination in the study of human communication. Human communication is the *sine qua non* of any field of inquiry and yet no common set of terms and taxonomy has been developed. No outside framework or model exists by which the discoveries in various fields can be uniformly examined and tested.

The articles in the book look at this phenomenon from many angles: zoology, anthropology, general semantics, general system theory, neurophysiology, symbolic interaction, and the sociology of knowledge. Since the book was intended to help promote the creation of a new field of study, there is no conclusion, but as with *Maps of the Mind* it does engender perspective taking.

These two books — *Maps of the Mind* and *Interdisciplinary Approach to Human Communication* — attempt to take a "meta" position to their fields of inquiry. Such a position is like the one taken in ethics when deliberation is done about ethical thinking. Such activity is called "metaethics." One can also take a meta position to transformation as well. Such a position is active and deals with the transformation of the form of transformation or "metamorphosis." Questions about faith from both of these meta positions will now be raised.

When *Life Maps* is viewed from a meta position many ancient traps are exposed. The first has to do with reification or not turning faith into a thing. The second has to do with making equivalent comparisons between faith models. The third warning relates to using an appropriate amount of precision for one's analysis of faith.

The temptation to turn faith into a substance or thing creates a static basis of comparison and analysis. The faith process and the system in which it functions as well as the model's relationship to the subsystem and suprasystem related to it would be missed if such a mistake were made.

If one wishes to treat faith as if it exists independently of its concept and name, then, one needs to be aware that a position is taken with the Realists. This position reaches back to the Neo-Platonists and to Plato himself. It is a tradition with the slogan, *universalia ante rem,* in medieval philosophy.

The opposite position to Realism is Nominalism. It reaches back, perhaps, to Aristotle, but it got its name from Roscellinus (d. 1122) who took an extreme stand against the reality of the Trinity based on the principles of nominalism. His argument was that there are three gods in the Trinity, because universals, such as "Trinity," are names of abstractions and abstractions have no reality outside of the mind of the thinker holding them. The slogan for this tradition was *universalia post rem.* Roscellinus' statement from which the Nominalists were named was *universalia sunt nomina* (universals are names).

A mediating position between the more Platonic Realists and more Aristotelian Nominalists was articulated by William of Ockham (d. 1349) and was called the *via moderna.* This position was also based on Aristotle but argued that thought is not the measure of reality. It is the means for interpreting human experience. Knowledge is a sign that stands for objects in the world. A slogan of this group might be *de universalibus pro individuis*.

The discussion in a modern key is much like the discussion we had above about the status of models and their relationship with reality. It also has to do with the modern view of reality as being best modeled by systemic patterns. This classical version of the controversy is helpful to be aware of as one ponders the contribution of faith to meaning.

The second warning is about matching up levels of analysis and component parts of models when making comparisons. Levels of abstraction leave out more and more details as each step is taken beyond what Alfred Korzybski called the "mad dance of electrons." Korzybski, a Polish mathematician and engineer, developed a point of view about the use of language called "General Semantics"[65] during the 1920s and '30s. His famous statement that "the map is not the territory" reminds us also that comparing equivalent levels of models still may not put us in touch with our own experience of faith's journey.

The third warning is to be wary of being too "scientific" in an unthinking and/or overprecise way. The real question is not whether to be scientific or not. It is how to be appropriately precise. Aristotle warned us against laying too strong an emphasis on precision as an end in itself in the *Nicomachean Ethics.* He said, "It is the mark of a properly trained mind to look for a degree of precision that is appropriate to the subject matter, and only to the extent that the nature of each allows."[66]

With these three warnings in mind we can continue. Fowler abstracted his view of faith from reports of many persons who were involved in the guided interviews his method prescribed. Keen stressed keeping close to the physical sensation of faith himself and attempting to get "inside" of its relational quality. Fowler stated his interest in the subtitle to *Stages of Faith* as "The Psychology of Human Development and the Quest for Meaning." Keen stated his interest in the title of his later book, *The Passionate Life.* The question now is what does a meta position of these two approaches and one's own personal approach show about faith and life?

One approach to this discussion is very ancient. It deals with the controversy that pitted faith and reason against each other as two forms of knowing. In the Introduction to *Life Maps* there was a reference to the "historical echoes" to be heard in the Fowler-Keen conversation (p. 2). There was also a reference to the "knowing-trusting" quality in the pattern of faith development (pp. 10–11). This controversy was glossed over by the hyphen and the quotation marks joining and guarding that term, "knowing-trusting."

The controversy was quite explicit in the third century. Tertullian (c. 160–230) focused on faith from the Latin tradition. He said that faith was the most appropriate way to know God. He trusted faith and asked the question, "What has Jerusalem to do with Athens?" Clement of Alexandria (150–215) took the opposite position and considered that philosophy was the handmaid of theology. He even argued that God gave pagan philosophy to the Greeks to prepare the way for the Gospel, as God had given the Law to the Jews for such a preparatory task. His language and culture was Greek rather than Latin.

Thomas Aquinas (1225–1274) lived in an age of synthesis. He argued a compromise position. The intellect was darkened by the Fall but it is not totally blind. One can, therefore, use both reason and faith but they must be used appropriately. The unaided intellect can grasp many truths about God by analogy with the created order, but doctrines such as the Trinity are known by faith from direct revelation.

In the Reformation of the sixteenth century the most influential theologian after Luther was John Calvin (1509–1564). He argued that one had to use Scripture as the measure of truth because of the total depravity of the intellect. It was completely blinded to God by sin, so faith and the interpretation of Scripture with the aid of the Holy Spirit was the only way to true knowledge.

In the seventeenth century the Copernican crack in the cosmic egg broke completely open and the new cosmic system was created in terms of mechanical laws which worked on earth and in heaven alike. This was an age when faith lost authority as a means of knowing. Few spoke in positive terms about the irrational aspect of religion. Pascal (1623–1662) is an example of someone who attempted to use both faith and reason equally in this difficult period. He argued that if we submit to reason totally then we will lose the mystery and supernatural quality of religion. On the other hand, if we cast out the principles of reason to be ruled by the heart, then we risk becoming absurd and ridiculous.

One might note that reason was used in defense of faith by Pascal. Somewhat the same phenomenon can be seen in another transition character, John Locke (1632–1704). He said that he believed in divine revelation but then he went on to argue that critical judgment about what revelation was saying required one to depend on reason to evaluate the faithful conclusion.

As we have already discussed above, the eighteenth century was a time when the importance of art and religion diminished. The Newtonian world of science and the moral universe of humankind prevailed. There were no categories by which to express the transcendent dimensions of and the knowing represented by faith. Evidences in the natural order of God, evidences in Scripture of miracles and prophecies which suspended the natural order, and evidence of obscurity in Scripture as in nature — all pointed to God, the Creator, the Christian defenders said. Science and religion had become contestants for total knowledge, but reason was unable to defend religion on the grounds it had pitched the battle. Faith and reason were driven apart again in this new version of Tertullian and Clement with the weight of science added to philosophy on the side of reason versus faith as the means to discover the truth about reality.

In the nineteenth century there was a reaction against the narrow use of the imagination, as we have also said above, and one of those who attacked the overconfidence in reason was Sören Kierkegaard (1813–1855). He argued that one had to literally jump from one context of knowing into another one to have faith. One had to leave behind the values of beauty and morality as the ultimate guides to knowing and make a leap of faith to experience religion.

This brings our story to a close once again at the time of the twentieth century. Today we do not assume that faith and reason are in opposition, but we are still attempting to discover what faith is. To do this we are using both reason and science. The question that this raises again, however, is whether or not this is appropriate.

The controversy about faith and reason, as it is put in terms of competing kinds of knowledge, seems beyond resolution. This is not the first time such a puzzle has existed in the life of thought. Another example from the history of ideas is the controversy between the subjective and objective views of value. This problem prompted Risieri Frondizi to write a book called *What Is Value?*[67]

The position of subjectivism asserted that value cannot be entirely divorced from valuation, but it is a mistake to reduce value to such projections. The objectivism position argued in response that values are independent of value objects and of the subjects who value them. They are absolute and unchangeable and cannot be affected by any actual physical or human event.

The overstatement of the objectivism position is an overreaction to the errors of subjectivism, but no philosophical school can be erected on the errors of an opposing doctrine. Both sides seemed to make statements that are partially true and both positions make the mistake of considering one aspect of the problem to the exclusion of others.

Frondizi's solution was to say that value is complex, so one must avoid reductionism on either the subjectivism or objectivism side. The whole configuration must be considered in a Gestalt so the true qualities of value can emerge.

Frondizi found that value is its own entity. It is neither a sum of the parts or an aggregate. It is a totality which is a synthesis of the objective and subjective contributions which exist and have meaning only in concrete human situations. Things and acts are valuable because we value them and because they are valuable in their own right.

The value controversy was locked into its conflict because of the way the positions were stated. It took Frondizi's reframing to solve its dilemma. The faith controversy is also locked into its positions by the way they are stated. When we ask, is it better to use faith or reason to know reality, we must know the answer before we know how to begin the investigation. To know the reality of either faith or reason we need to know which means is better to be used to find out.

Frondizi used Gestalt psychology to reframe the value

question. To solve the faith controversy we need to add a further element and it is dynamic. It is the model of fiduciary knowing created by Michael Polanyi.[68]

Polanyi argued from Gestalt psychology as did Frondizi, but he went a step beyond the more mechanical view of perception in that concept. According to the theory of Gestalt psychology[69] we know the coherence or pattern of an object by a spontaneous equilibration of visual clues or stimuli that are impressed on the retina or the brain. We may be unaware of these particulars or clues themselves but we know them in the object that we recognize or the activity that we do. What Polanyi added was the active involvement of the person in such knowing. The shaping or integrating power of the individual is "the great and indispensable tacit power by which all knowledge is discovered and, once discovered, is held to be true."[70]

The problem that one concentrates on is called the focal target by Polanyi. Clues, however, are coming into the tacit awareness at the same time. The clues become conscious in bits and pieces. Finally, when the focal target and the subsidiary clues are linked, the whole pattern is known consciously.

One cannot be aware of the focal and subsidiary knowing at the same time. This is why there is always a tacit dimension to our knowing. For the subsidiary knowing to work well one must give up one's self to the problem and pour himself or herself into it. There is in fact a fiduciary quality to all knowing because of this.

In *Personal Knowledge*[71] Polanyi identified the parallel between the process of scientific discovery and the Pauline conversion experience and scheme of redemption. The Christian pursues an unattainable goal, the creative relationship with God, by an act of faith aided by grace. The scientist surrenders his or her efforts to a difficult and important problem and is visited by an understanding that seems beyond realization. This means that the fiduciary framework includes doubt as well as belief in knowing. Both are components of knowing but do not undermine the process unless commitment to doubt shuts down the fiduciary part of the process.

Polanyi gives us a conceptual model by which to better understand the statement of "reciprocal causality" identified by Maurice Blondel in Augustine's work and mentioned in the Introduction of *Life Maps* (p. 10). Augustine's paradoxical phrases *crede ut intelligas* and *intellige ut credas* are joined together in the reciprocal process of tacit knowing in this way.

The question about Fowler and Keen that this discussion raises is whether or not we might join their ways of discovery together into a diagram such as the one used by Richard Gelwick to illustrate Polanyi's theory of tacit knowing:[72]

The appearance of the pattern of faith development is the phenomenal aspect. The meaning of the pattern put into words is the semantic aspect. How this pattern and meaning bear on the way one knows and lives is the final aspect. These levels all function at once but we have different amounts of awareness of them at different times and places.

Fowler and Keen are involved in focal and subsidiary knowing at all three levels. Fowler prefers or has a tendency toward stressing focal knowing while Keen is more attracted to subsidiary knowing. Fowler is more engaged with the semantic aspect and Keen is more involved with the phenomenal aspect. Both are aware of the ontological implications of their faith, but the ways they have of working this out and expressing it differ.

One must continue with this line of investigation to ask

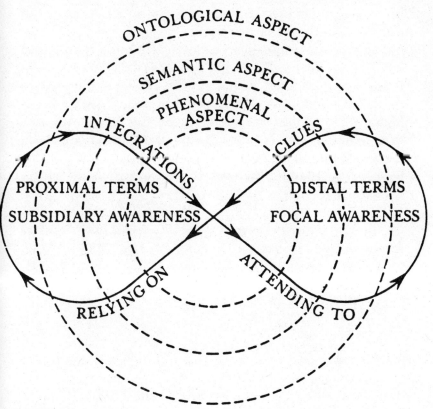

Figure 4.1
Diagram of Tacit Knowing

you, the reader, where you fit in this epistemological model. What do you prefer? Can you begin to explore what your model for faith is like? To do this is to become involved in the changing of one's transformational process, so the question is important and takes some care to answer. When one conceptualizes his or her faith model one's life is changed by making such a judgment even if the result of the judgment is only a platform from which to move on toward other views of one's journey.

The transformational process by which one's faith model will link up the focal knowing with the subsidiary knowing is the creative process applied to this problem. The pattern of this transformational process has been outlined by James Loder.[73] He applied the literature on the creative process to theological concerns. Both Loder and Polanyi have used the experience of St. Paul on the Damascus Road as a theological case study for their respective conclusions which are similar.

The pattern by which one can expect to change to know one's own transformational process on the faith journey can be outlined by using a combination of Loder and Polanyi to say that the pattern is as follows:

1. *Awareness of the Problem*
   The focal point is how to create a model for faith development.
2. *Scanning for a Solution to the Problem*
   The interplay of the focal and subsidiary knowing continues in a tacit way.
3. *The Intuition of a Solution*
   The pattern and its meaning are linked to the focal knowing. A shift of energy from scanning to working out an articulated answer is felt.
4. *Articulation of the Solution*
   The pattern is put together in semantic terms.
5. *Reality Testing*
   The semantic awareness is tested against the reality experience of others.

People have different tendencies toward different parts of this model of transformation as they do toward parts of Polanyi's model of knowing. We might say that Fowler has spent a great deal more time and energy on the fourth and fifth aspect of his discovery of a faith model than Keen has. Keen, on the other hand, seems to be drawn toward the finding of problems, scanning, and the delight of the intuition of a possible solution. He is more likely than Fowler to move on to a new problem before working out its articulation and testing. You will be drawn toward different parts of this pattern as well.

This brings to a close the raising of questions about how Fowler and Keen relate to the faith and reason controversy and the translations of it into new keys. We turn now to the third and last part of this section. How does your faith model compare to Fowler's and Keen's with respect to tools, the cartographer factor, the usefulness of the developmental image and one's own meta position about all three models — Fowler's, Keen's, and the reader's?

These questions are organized in the same way that the sections of this chapter are organized. We will begin with questions about the appropriate tools to be used to make a map of faith.

1. Does the word, "faith," point to something symbolic or is it to be used as a sign?
2. Is the phenomenon referred to by the word, "faith," a simple entity or is it a compound entity which involves both component parts and the relations among the parts?
3. Is the model for the faith entity a dynamic system? Is the system open or closed?
4. Is the faith model one that involves the whole human being in a way that prevents the whole faith process from being conscious at one time? Must one have faith in faith to study it?
5. What kind of evidence is appropriate to further understand this phenomenon? How does the paradigm one is using form the criteria for defining a "fact"?

These questions and the ones which follow are not perfect. It may be that they are not phrased in a way appropriate for you. At least, one can use the general categories of tools, cartographers, maps, and mapping maps to formulate your own enquiry.

The second group of questions are collected around the topic of cartographer. In general they focus on the training and trustworthy qualities of the map-maker.

1. What kind of training is appropriate for a faith cartographer?
2. Are the patterns in faith mapping confined to patterns in human language? Can a cartographer place meaning that goes beyond human language on a map?
3. What does biblical language have to do with mapping faith?
4. Is biblical language "improved" by translating it into theological, psychological, sociological, anthropological, or some other logical framework?
5. Must one be one's own cartographer? Comment on the following poem excerpt with respect to this question:

> But thou at home, without tide or gale
> Canst in thy map securely sail,
> Seeing those painted countries, and so guess
> By those fine shades their substances;
> And from thy compass taking small advice
> By'st travel at the lowest price.[74]

This brings us to the last set of questions by which an upward spiral toward a meta position might be taken. With these this last chapter will draw to a close.

1. How do Fowler, Keen, and you differ in the way you use symbols, models, and paradigms?
2. What can be learned from Fowler's or Keen's maps that can't be learned from the other one and what does your map include that neither of theirs does?

3. What does Fowler's map, Keen's map, and your map have in common?
4. What is the best use that each of the three maps can be put to?
5. At what point in the creative process are you most likely to get stuck? What about Fowler? Keen?

There is only one way that a "Non-Concluding Postscript" can end. It is with a wish to all who are on the way that their journey of knowing and being be a graceful one.

The End and the Beginning

Endnotes

1. Ian Barbour, *Myths, Models and Paradigms: A Comparative Study on Science and Religion* (New York: Harper and Row, 1974).

2. This discussion was primarily begun by Thomas S. Kuhn in *The Structure of Scientific Revolutions* (Chicago: University of Chicago Press, 1962). Since 1962 he has modified his views to be less sweeping and more precise. For comment from a theologian please see Sallie McFague's book *Metaphorical Thinking* (Philadelphia: Fortress Press, 1982) with special reference to pp. 79–83 and note 29 on p. 209.

3. Referred to by Lloyd A. Brown, *The Story of Maps* (Boston: Little, Brown, 1949), p. 34, and in *The Mapmakers* by John Noble Wilford (New York: Alfred A. Knopf, Inc., 1981), p. 12. The *Variae Historiae* is a third century document.

4. The term, "Cartophobia," was introduced to this author by Dr. Robert Tucker in his thesis which this author supervised. Please see David Greenhood, *Mapping* (Chicago: University of Chicago Press, 1964).

5. These two maps may be found in Colin McEvedy, *The Penguin Atlas of Medieval History* (Harmondsworth, Middlesex, England: Penguin Books, 1962).

6. Ian Barbour, *Myths, Models and Paradigms,* pp. 34–48.

7. Sallie McFague, *Metaphorical Theology: Models of Gods in Religious Language* (Philadelphia: Fortress Press, 1982), pp. 83–90.

8. Barbour and McFague have contributed greatly to this summary. McFague especially contributed #6 and #7. The comparison, however, is not limited to their views.

9. Ian Barbour, *Myths, Models and Paradigms,* p. 9.

10. Thomas S. Kuhn, *The Structure of Scientific Revolutions,* 2nd ed. (Chicago: University of Chicago Press, 1970). The second edition included a Postscript to clarify his views.

11. Thomas Kuhn, "Second Thoughts on Paradigms" in *The Structure of Scientific Theories,* ed., Frederick Suppe (Urbana, Illinois: University of Illinois Press, 1977). A summary of Kuhn's chapter may be found in McFague, *Metaphorical Theology,* p. 80.

12. Examples of these dissertations are: Eugene Mischey, Ph.D., diss., University of Toronto, 1976; Sharon Parks, Ph.D., diss.

Harvard University, 1980; Richard Shulik, Ph.D., diss. University of Chicago, 1979.

13. Walter Conn, "Affectivity in Kohlberg and Fowler" *Religious Education,* 76 (January–February 1981).

14. Eugene J. Mischey, "Faith, Identity, and Morality in Late Adolescence," *Character Potential: A Record of Research* IX (November, 1981).

15. Professor Dr. Karl Ernst Nipkow, "Wachstum Des Glaubens-Stufen Des Glaubens," *Reformation und Praktische Theologies,* H. M. Müller and D. Rööoler, eds., Festshrift für W. Jettei (Göttingen: n.p., 1983).
    An international conference of note was published in *Toward Moral and Religious Maturity,* Christiane Brusselmans, ed., (Morristown, N.J.: Silver Burdett Co., 1980). The senior authors for the Conference were James W. Fowler and Antoine Vergote. The Conference was held at the Abbey of Senanque during a week in the spring of 1979 in Southern France.

16. Gabriel Moran, *Religious Education Development: Images for the Future* (Minneapolis: Winston Press, 1983).

17. Faith Development in the Adult Life Cycle, Kenneth Stokes, Director/Administrator, 9709 Rich Road, Minneapolis, MN 55437.

18. Sam Keen, *Apology for Wonder* (New York: Harper and Row, 1969).

19. Carol Gilligan, *In a Different Voice* (Cambridge: Harvard University, 1982).

20. Erik Erikson, *Insight and Responsibility: Lectures on the Ethical Implications of Psychoanalytic Insight* (New York: Norton, 1964).

21. Erik H. Erikson, *Childhood and Society* (New York: Norton, 1950). An excellent review of this book's achievement may be found in Robert Cole's *Erik H. Erikson: The Growth of His Work* (Boston: Little, Brown and Co., 1970). A discussion of the life cycle may be found in Paul Roazen, *Erik H. Erikson: The Power and Limits of a Vision* (New York: The Free Press, 1976), see especially pp. 107–120.

22. Wallace B. Clift, *Jung and Christianity: The Challenge of Reconciliation* (New York: Crossroads Publishing Co., 1983).

23. Michael Fordham, *The Life of Childhood* (London: Kegan Paul, Trench, Trubner and Co., Ltd., 1944). A new revised edition was published as *Children As Individuals* in 1969 in England and

in the U.S.A. in 1970 (New York: C. G. Jung Foundation for Analytical Psychology, Inc., 1970).

24. James W. Fowler, *Stages of Faith: The Psychology of Human Development and the Quest for Meaning* (San Francisco: Harper and Row, 1981).

25. James W. Fowler, Personal Communication, 13 September, 1984.

26. David E. Roberts, *Existentialism and Religious Belief,* ed., Roger Hazelton (New York: Oxford University Press, 1957), p. 279.

27. Paul Arthur Schilpp and Lewis Edwin Hahn, eds., *The Philosophy of Gabriel Marcel* (La Salle, Illinois: Open Court, 1984).

28. Sam Keen, "The Development of the Idea of Being in Marcel's Thought," *The Philosophy of Gabriel Marcel,* pp. 99–121, and Sam Keen, *Gabriel Marcel* (Richmond, Virginia: John Knox Press, 1967).

29. David E. Roberts, *Existentialism and Religious Belief,* pp. 280–281.

30. Sam Keen, *To a Dancing God* (New York: Harper and Row, 1970).

31. Ibid., p. 99.

32. David E. Roberts, *Existentialism and Religious Belief,* pp. 280–281.

33. Gabriel Marcel, *The Mystery of Being,* 2 vols. (Chicago: Henry Regnery, 1951).

34. Sam Keen and Anne Valley Fox, *Telling Your Story: A Guide to Who You Are and Who You Can Be* (New York: Doubleday and Company, 1974).

35. Sam Keen, *The Passionate Life: Stages of Loving* (San Francisco: Harper and Row, 1983), p. 35.

36. Paul Ricoeur, "Gabriel Marcel and Phenomenology," in *The Philosophy of Gabriel Marcel,* pp. 471–495.

37. Sam Keen, *Voices and Visions* (San Francisco: Harper and Row, 1974), p. 107.

38. Edward Farley, *Ecclesial Man* (Philadelphia: Fortress Press, 1975). The reference to method vs. attitude is at pp. 28–29. This book includes not only the study of Husserl and his program but mainly is a study of the pre-criteriological (criteria being Scripture, tradition, etc.) situation of faith. It is a study of the problem of reality that pushes theological method (criteriology) back to the pre-criteria situation in which realities are immediately grasped. It is, therefore, a social phenomenology of faith and reality.

39. Sam Keen, *Apology for Wonder*, pp. 21–40.

40. Sam Keen, *Gabriel Marcel*, pp. 13–16.

41. Jean Piaget, *Insights and Illusions of Philosophy*, 2nd ed., (New York: World Publishing Co., 1971).

42. Sam Keen, "The Development of the Idea of Being In Marcel's Thought" in *The Philosophy of Gabriel Marcel*.

43. Horace Freeland Judson, *The Search for Solutions* (New York: Holt, Rinehart and Winston, 1980). Please see especially Chapter 2.

44. Gerhard Von Rad, *Genesis. A Commentary* (Philadelphia: The Westminster Press, 1961), pp. 277–282.

45. John Dillenberger, *Protestant Thought and Natural Science: A Historical Interpretation of the Issues Behind the 500-Year-Old Debate* (Garden City, New York: Doubleday and Co., 1960). See pp. 23 and 26 for examples of the use of this elegant phrase.

46. E. M. W. Tillyard, *The Elizabethan World Picture* (New York: Macmillan, n.d.).

47. Sallie McFague, *Metaphorical Theology*, p. 77. Her discussion in turn relies on Mary B. Hess, *Science and the Human Imagination* (London: SCM Press, 1954).

48. Thomas M. King, *Teilhard's Mysticism of Knowing* (New York: Seabury Press, 1981). The word, "groping," is discussed on pp. 32–33 and in note 1 of Chapter 2 on p. 150.

49. Gail Sheehy, *Passages* (New York: Dutton, 1976).

50. George Vaillant, *Adaptation of Life* (Boston: Little, Brown, 1977).

51. Daniel Levinson, *The Seasons of a Man's Life* (New York: Knopf, 1978).

52. Roger Gould, *Transformations* (New York: Simon and Schuster, 1978).

53. Bernard Boelen, *Personal Maturity* (New York: Seabury, 1978).

54. Gabriel Moran, *Religious Education Development*, pp. 43–44, and 90–93.

55. Bernice Neugarten, et al., *Personality and Later Life* (New York: Atherton, 1964).

56. Marjorie Fiske Lowenthal, et al., *Four States of Life* (San Francisco: Jossey-Bass, 1976).

57. Carol Gilligan, *In a Different Voice*.

58. Sam Keen, *The Passionate Life*. The perversity of normality is described pp. 114–122 and how the outlaw breaks out of

the stereotypes of the warfare between the sexes is pp. 150–167.

59. Ibid., pp. 27–33. This is a statement of method.

60. Gabriel Moran, *Religious Education Development.*

61. Jerome Kagan, *The Nature of the Child* (New York: Basic Books, 1984).

62. Ibid., p. xiv and all of Chapter 3.

63. Charles Hampden-Turner, *Maps of the Mind: Charts and Concepts of the Mind and Its Labyrinths* (New York: Macmillan, 1981).

64. Richard W. Budd and Brent D. Ruben, eds., *Interdisciplinary Approaches to Human Communication* (Rochelle Park, New Jersey: Hayden Book Company, Inc., 1979).

65. Alfred Korzybski, *Science and Sanity,* 3rd ed., (Lakeville, Conn: The International Non-Aristotelian Library Publishing Co., 1948). The first edition of this work in English was by Dutton in 1933.

66. Aristotle, *Nicomachean Ethics,* 1.3. 10946. 19.

67. Risieri Frondizi, *What Is Value?* 2nd ed., (LaSalle, Illinois: Open Court Publishing Co., 1971).

68. A good introduction to Polanyi's work which includes its relation to theology and to science may be found in Richard Gelwick's book, *The Way of Discovery: An Introduction to the Thought of Michael Polanyi* (New York: Oxford University Press, 1977).

69. Max Wertheimer's paper on apparent movement in 1912 consolidated the Gestalt approach as against using the sensation as a unit of consciousness and for conceptualizing mental processes as dynamic, structural units with unique properties which are lost in introspective analysis. Kurt Koffka and Wolfgang Kohler are also associated with the early Gestalt movement in psychology.

70. Michael Polanyi, *The Tacit Dimension* (Garden City: Doubleday, 1966), p. 6.

71. Michael Polanyi, *Personal Knowledge: Towards a Post-Critical Philosophy* (Chicago: University of Chicago Press, 1958), p. 324.

72. Richard Gelwick, *The Way of Discovery,* p. 77.

73. James Loder, *The Transforming Moment* (San Francisco: Harper and row, 1981).

74. Robert Herrick, quoted in David Greenwood, *Mapping,* p. xii.